Angel Over My Shoulder

W9-AAP-406

Angel Over My Shoulder

40 True Stories of Angelic Encounters

Barb Karg and Rick Sutherland

FAIR WINDS
PRESS
GLOUCESTER, MASSACHUSETTS

Text © 2004 by Barb Karg and Rick Sutherland

First published in the USA in 2004 by
Fair Winds Press
33 Commercial Street
Gloucester, MA 01930

All rights reserved. No part of this book may be
reproduced or utilized, in any form or by any
means, electronic or mechanical, without prior
permission in writing from the publisher.

08 07 06 05 04   1 2 3 4 5

ISBN 1-59233-053-3

Library of Congress Cataloging-in-Publication
Data available

Cover design by Ariana Grabec-Dingman
Book design and layout by Barb Karg

Printed and bound in Canada

This book is dedicated to our extraordinary family members, who continually touch our lives and our hearts: Ma, Pop, Dale, Dottie, Chrissy, Kathy, Anne, and Terry Bob. We love you all.

It is also a tribute to all our wonderful friends, who, whether they know it or not, are all angels in disguise.

And to Rebecca Sutherland and Rosalia Fisch, we pay special tribute. Never a day goes by when we don't think about you. We know you're watching. And we know you're proud.

Table of Contents

Table of Contents

Introduction

Guardian angels. Do they exist?

Are they entities we can see and feel, or just mere figments of imaginations subconsciously influenced by religion, literary works, television, and philosophical upbringing? Is their presence divine, practical, logical, or circumstantial? Are they ever-present, or do they show up only during times of extreme joy or stress?

When we first came up with the idea for this book, we had myriad discussions about guardian angels. They reminded us of all things personal, professional, religious, domestic, international, universal—you name it. Our visions ranged from haloed harp-playing cherubs to unseen divine forces to red-capped crime fighters in major cities.

What started as a fascination with a subject that many find esoteric, unconventional, and perhaps even unbelievable, became a journey into lives, loves, strength, courage, heartbreak, and triumph of the human spirit and the power that faith and the fates have on our being.

Stripped of its trees, the forest is a barren wasteland; without stars, the night sky becomes an intimidating abyss; without tides, the oceans recede to arid desert sands. So it is in the presence of angels. Like the course of nature, they nourish, replenish, and fill our souls with life. The air we breathe is a gift. The angel who comes to us in a breeze reminds us of that gift. The angel who comes to light the way during a dark journey offers hope and promise. The angel who baptizes us during the greatest of storms clears our minds and enables us to see with better eyes.

For many people, the existence of angels remains elusive. Is it because those individuals are afraid to open their minds to the very possibility? Is the thought of such an entity or power too much for them to accept on moral or religious grounds? Or could it be that angels are no more real to them than Bigfoot or the Loch Ness monster?

In a world filled with turmoil, chaos, war, indifference, ignorance, prejudice, poverty, and hunger, has there never been a time when you took a step back and thought, why is this happening? And amid all those stories of tragedy and triumph, have you never had cause to wonder how some miraculous turnaround occurred?

Although it's true that the scientific, religious, and philosophical communities will never agree on the subject of angels or divine intervention, it's also true that, as individuals, we will never agree on their presence. In our travels, however, we've come across many people from all three communities and states of mind who have had experiences they cannot explain. Without proof to the contrary, we surmise, the presence of guardian angels cannot be disputed. They can exist.

But, we ask, does it really matter? Isn't it enough just knowing that their existence is a possibility? People believe in all manner of things—past lives, pet rocks, alien abduction, that green M&Ms make one frisky. The list is endless. Yet the beauty of the variety in humanity is just that—we're allowed to be different in our opinions and beliefs, and if not for those differences, the world would be a controlled utopia under glass. We'd all breathe the same air, abide by the same rules, listen to the same concertos, and be void of the pleasures of playful debate.

So the legacy of guardian angels lives on in those of us who've had encounters, or reason to believe we've had encounters, with something out of the ordinary. What we found most delightful and intriguing about the submissions we received from all our wonderful contributors is the diversity of their experiences and the journeys that brought them to where they are today. Again, these are the experiences that illuminate the beautiful variety of the human species.

If there is something to be learned by reading the prose contained within these pages, it's that guardian angels come in many forms and deliver myriad messages, from the blatant to the sublime. They speak or act, and we listen and notice— sometimes not hard enough, and sometimes with too close an ear. Fortunately for us, their presence has always offered a sense of peace and comfort, relieved pain and sorrow, soothed our taunted minds, and set us on the right path—all without adding to the burden of our typically hectic, and sometimes traumatic, existences. The individuals who've contributed to this anthology have confronted the subject of angels in various ways. Their tales are intelligent, humorous, philo- sophical, and in some cases tragic, but they always come from the heart. We'd like to think that the unused portions of our gray matter are in reserve for the miraculous wonders that future individuals will be fortunate enough to witness.

For now, though, we should be content knowing that there are powers much greater than us, and that with each passing day, with each sunrise, and with each new breath, we are one step closer to achieving a measure of serenity. If that peace comes in the form of an angel, so be it. Never are we more alive than when we're broadening our minds and growing as a result of that action. If we had the luxury of immortality, we might well see the fruits of our current intellectual labor.

Until then, however, we'll have to be content in knowing that for each seemingly unexplainable occurrence in life there exists the possibility of divine intervention. For us, that's enough, as it is for the millions of individuals who feel their lives have been blessed in some small measure at some point along the way. We hope you enjoy these experiences, and in reading them feel inspired and touched. Through love, laughter, and tears, the human spirit endures, now and long after we're gone.

—*Barb Karg and Rick Sutherland*

Where Mothers Fear to Tread

by Cindy Robert

My son thinks I am fearless. I can check under beds for monsters, and I am not afraid of bogeymen who might be lurking in the closet waiting to pounce. I have even been known to walk into a dark room without turning on a single light! And if Daddy isn't home, I can dispense with a spider in the blink of an eye.

Because of these, and other valiant deeds he has seen me perform, he thinks that nothing scares me. He couldn't be more wrong. I outgrew being afraid of things that go bump in the night, only to have that fear turn into something much more terrifying, something I acquired when I became a mom. It starts even before your first child is born. You worry with irrational fears, consoling yourself that it will all be okay once the baby is born, once you can see him, once he is placed in your arms where he can be protected and immune to anything bad. Of course, your worrying doesn't go away then. It is just the beginning, and it continues to grow right along with your child. You can almost use the same "Watch Me Grow" chart that is taped to the wall to measure it! You have the unexplained fevers in the middle of the night, the cuts and bruises, and the "I just turned my back for a minute . . ." experiences.

With three kids I thought I had gone through it all, that I had faced my worst nightmares. But I was wrong. Nothing had prepared me for the day that my son, Tommy, came up missing.

He was riding his bike out front when he noticed his friends were outside and asked if he could go down to their house to play. I walked to the end of our driveway and saw the two boys with Alicia, their mother, playing in their front yard. Being too far away to call to, I waved until I got her attention. She waved back, as was our signal that children were on the way. I told Tommy to go ahead, and reminded him to stay out of the street and to be good, along the rest of the litany of precautions I recited to him on a daily basis. I watched until he reached the boys and their mother, then I went back inside to start dinner.

Usually, I would have let him play there until dinnertime, when I would call on the phone or send my oldest daughter, Lauren, down to get him. For some reason, after ten minutes or so, I decided to walk down and check on him. While I was still a house away, I saw the boys and their mother, but not my son.

Thinking he had gone inside to use the bathroom, or maybe was getting something from the backyard, I wasn't alarmed. Still, something started inside of me.

"Where is Tommy?" I asked.

Alicia said, "He was here just a minute ago. Guys, have you seen Tommy?"

The something started to grow as the two boys said they didn't know where he had gone. He couldn't have just disappeared, could he? I started knocking on all the nearby houses that had a child he knew. I was running by the time I had worked my way back home. I stayed only long enough to tell Lauren to watch her little sister, Grace, grab my keys, and run back out the door. I drove around the block and wanted to go further, but I kept remembering what I'd heard and read about missing children and calling 911 as soon as possible—how every minute counts, and how every minute you lose . . .

Trying to silence the path my thoughts were taking, I sped home, grabbed the cordless phone, and punched in 911 as I went back outside, searching again as far as the connection allowed.

I'm a writer, and I like to think that I have a decent command of the written word, but mere words, no matter how you manipulate them, cannot begin to describe how I felt at that moment. I can tell you of the horrific thoughts that were snaking through my head to my heart. I can tell you how I tried to stay calm as I described for the operator the clothes my son was wearing the last time I had seen him. I can tell you the details, but never can I describe the immense fear I felt.

I was unable to go far, tied to the cordless phone connection as I was. All I could do was hang on as the 911 operator had instructed, while trying to fight back the tears as I gave even more information, silently praying to whomever would listen. I felt as though the cement of the sidewalk was holding me in place, keeping me from my son, when Alicia drove by in her car.

"Where do you want me to look?" she asked.

"Dromedary Court," I replied.

I thought that Tommy might have gone to an older friend's house. He had asked me numerous times if he could, but I always said no because it was the next block over. That street was named Jaguar, but for some unknown reason I'd mistakenly said Dromedary Court, a street that was five blocks away. Certainly he couldn't, he wouldn't, have gone that far. Alicia's house was in the opposite direction, and he would have had to pass right by our house—our kitchen window—to get to the crossroad. I tried to call her back to tell her my mistake, but she had already gone.

Minutes later I saw her car turn the corner. It was almost dark by then, and I couldn't see into the windows, but I noticed the trunk was open with what appeared to be the handlebars of a bicycle sticking out—Tommy's bike. I let the air I had been holding captive in my chest free. She had found him.

He had ridden to Dromedary Court, and he had done so without passing our house. It seems that there were vacant lots on every street from ours to where he had gone, and they all pretty much lined up. His excuse? He didn't have a good one, he just wanted to ride his bike, and since I didn't like him riding on the road or on neighbors' lawns, he thought he would ride through the empty lots.

For the most part, he has already forgotten the whole incident. I haven't and never will. As the weeks have slipped into months, I remember the fear that now grips me a little less, and the thankfulness and wonder for the guardian angel who brought him home safely.

Cindy Robert lives with her husband and three children in Florida. When not writing, she spends her time doing battle with weeds and uninvited visitors in what she likes to think of as a garden.

In the Arms of an Angel

by Mary Hall-Marshall

*T*he only sound in the silent emergency bay was my sobbing. My daughter, Judy, hovering near death, tried to console me in these last moments before she was taken away. I was inconsolable, unaware of anyone or anything other than the strong arm of my husband holding me upright, and the pale, dying figure on the gurney. The doors opened and a swarm of aqua scrubs rushed forward, grabbed the gurney, and broke into one of those dead runs you see in television movies. But this was real. This was my child, and the doctor had told us that they had only a thirty-minute window in which to save her. I grieved for my child, who was losing the transplant battle, her brother Mark's donated kidney, and perhaps her life. Even if she survived, she would be forced once again to let the dialysis machine take over her life.

Standing at the window in her hospital room, I looked out on the Dallas skyline. I remembered another day in this same hospital, looking over the same view of the city, thirty-five years earlier. On that day, I held a pink flannel blanket and let awe overcome me as I looked into the doll-like face of my first daughter. My young life had never known a more precious moment.

She was sweet with baby powder and her name, planned for three years, was Mary Angela, but we simply called her Angela. Her damp, black ringlets spoke of her paternal Comanche blood. Her dimples flashed across her cheeks, and her skin was creamy instead of ruddy like a newborn's usually is. When she opened her violet eyes, I was hopelessly captured. Her rose-petal hand clung to my forefinger like she would never let go, and I envisioned eventual ballet tutus, prom dresses, and wedding gowns.

"She doesn't look real," I stated over and over. Every mother thinks her babies are beautiful, but each family member and friend who saw her agreed—a sacred feeling of reverence hung in the air. This baby, less than six pounds, was special, and we all knew it. "I'm glad we named her Angela. She looks like an angel," said my husband.

"Did you know when I come for visiting hours, people are clustered in front of her, talking about how beautiful she is?"

Angela's isolette had been placed front and center behind the nursery windows. A nurse said it was because she looked like a miniature rosy-cheeked six-month-old. But deep down I knew our little girl was simply a visitor—that God had sent her into our lives on a short, unknown mission, and on the third day, without warning, she returned to her heavenly home. They said it was peritonitis. My heart was broken.

We buried her in an unmarked grave under the shade of a juniper tree. A family friend had provided a plot in the "baby land" of the cemetery, knowing we struggled financially in our young marriage. Her daddy said he could never bear to return, and soon after, we moved from the area. I felt cheated, bruised, and unfulfilled. The only solace was the thought,

God needed another angel. My greatest comfort was my son, Mark, with his huge amber eyes, who tried to keep his mommy from crying.

Ten months later, in June 1964, Judy was born. She was premature and sickly. Throughout her childhood, Judy was hospitalized and treated on a regular basis.

"We're simply buying time," her urologist told us. "If we can keep her clear of infection with dilations and careful observation, perhaps the kidney transplant will be perfected by the time she's grown."

For many years her kidney problem seemed to be in remission. Even the trauma of my break-up with her father did not slow her down. Judy tucked it into the back of her mind, and she excelled at ballet, trained for competitive gymnastics, and held the head cheerleader position in high school. In spite of the odds, she managed to live and function as well as any normal, pretty, energetic young woman.

Until she became pregnant with her first son. After his birth, she was advised not to have any more children, because of the complications she'd suffered. But she wanted her second son, and so he also was born.

On Memorial Day of Judy's thirtieth year, my second husband and I placed yellow roses on Angela's grave. As an act of love, my second husband had located her grave for me. More than 360 miles away, unbeknownst to us, at that very hour, Judy was in the emergency room being treated for a stroke caused by high blood pressure; in the vicious cycle set up by her congenital condition, high blood pressure was destroying her kidneys. The stroke was not light, but her recovery was swift.

Unfortunately, Judy's oldest son developed a rare kidney disease called glomerular sclerosis during this period. In a bad moment after a trip to the specialist in a distant city, Judy called one night. During our gloomy conversation, she said, "Mama, if Hunter dies, you're going to have to bury me right beside him." "Now, you stop that!" I said. "You're talking about MY child! And I've already lost one daughter!"

"I've always wondered how you survived that," she said.

"A mother never gets over the loss of a child," I replied. "A chunk of her heart is always missing. There are still times when I cry over it," I said, swiping at a tear.

"I've always longed for Angela, always wished I had that big sister to go with my big brother," Judy admitted.

I told Judy to explain to Hunter the importance of his guardian angel and that Grammy was praying for his angel to appear. After hanging up the phone, I went back to the computer. About one-thirty in the morning, the phone rang.

"Mama, I hope you weren't sleeping," Judy said. "I just had to call. I fell asleep praying and all of a sudden, the most beautiful angel was standing over me. She had long, black, wavy hair that trailed about five feet behind her. "I asked the girl who she was. 'I'm your guardian angel,' she told me. "I asked her to come closer so I could see her face. Mama, I can still feel her hands on my cheeks as she looked right into my eyes. Her eyes were wonderful—the most beautiful shade of violet I've ever seen. When I asked her what her name was, she whispered, 'Angela.'"

"Angela?" I couldn't believe it.

"I asked her if she was my sister, and she said 'yes'."

"My baby Angela?"

"I know it was her, Mama. I told her I'd always longed for her and she said, 'I've always been here.'"

Time passed and I wondered if it had all been just a dream Judy had, and I began to discount it all. But several weeks later, Judy's family came to visit. Judy took me aside for a moment alone.

"Mama, I've seen Angela again. She had a message for you, but I don't understand it. She said: 'Tell Mother I didn't hurt.'"

I was stunned. When Angela had died, I'd been tortured by the idea that my baby had suffered and I could do nothing about it. It was the one fear I'd never voiced to another soul—only God knew about it. And now Angela had told Judy that she had not suffered. A huge weight lifted from my heart, and I was filled with joy.

All these years later I am in another hospital room with my second beloved daughter. But this time I know I am not alone. Angela is with us. Just the thought of her gives me strength. I pray for Judy with Angela by my side. It has been a long, hard road for Judy.

She had her first kidney transplant in 1996, after being on dialysis for about a year. Hunter's illness was in miraculous remission, clearing the way for Judy to tend to her own health. That first kidney was accompanied by many trips to Dallas, and many more surgeries and complications, before she lost it fourteen months later. Once again, the dialysis machine kept her alive while we waited for another transplant. Judy's brother, Mark, tested for donation and was told he was a perfect match. So, the second transplant went forward almost three years after the first. It was this transplant that had brought Judy to the threshold of death once again when the kidney hemorrhaged.

We waited a long time. Finally the doctor came in. He had bad news for us. Not only did Judy lose her brother's gift of life, but she almost lost her own life as well. But, she'd pulled through, just barely. I smiled. With Angela's help, I knew Judy would survive. And she did.

Today, Judy approaches the fourth anniversary of her successful third kidney transplant, Hunter is doing well, and our lives have settled into a routine once again. I've had a lot of time to think about Angela. Somewhere along the way, a friend suggested that God had sent Angela into our lives to watch over our family and me. I believe she was right. We have always received unexpected blessings at the most tragic and the most wonderful times. We've witnessed more miracles than many families we know.

I'm the mother of an angel. I held and kissed an angel. My arms felt so empty when our angel went back home, but she has come back when we needed her. I know in my heart, that when I draw my last breath, she will be back—and I will fall into the arms of the angel I once cradled in my own baby.

Late some nights, as my husband and our three dogs sleep, and stillness settles in, I hear a soft, gentle sound. In my maternal heart, I know it's the rustle of wings.

Mary Hall-Marshall lives in North Texas with her husband, Wes, two Maltese cats, and a rescued Lhasa apso. A mother of four and grandmother of four, Mary is a freelance writer and also serves as the website development advisor for Daughters of the American Revolution. She loves needlework, reading, and family holidays.

In Search of Angels

by Susan Reynolds

A few years ago, my photography mentor encouraged me to stretch my imagination and suggested I photograph one object from every conceivable angle, in a variety of media. I spent a week experimenting with objects, but nothing gelled. I was one week away from deadline when a friend called and invited me to join her for a walk. She suggested a local cemetery, which featured acres of manicured hillsides with winding pathways. Toward the end of the day, just before we headed back to our cars, a bird flew perilously close to my head, causing me to turn sharply and catch first sight of a stunning angel statue behind a row of trees.

The area was the most secluded area in the cemetery, so secluded that I had to brush away tree branches to gain full view. The angel was tall and graceful and wore flowing robes and sandals. Her long windswept hair, her face lifted toward the sky, her hands clasped in prayer, and her aging fragility captivated me. Low hanging branches and thick cobwebs covered her, so I made note of where she was located and vowed to return the next day to unearth her. The next day, I brought along a pair of clippers, a brush, and a misting bottle.

I clipped tree limbs, brushed away the cobwebs, and misted away years of dust and grime while I whispered endearments, telling the angel how glad I was to have discovered her, how happy I felt restoring her to her original beauty, and how I wanted to photograph her so that others could experience her beauty. I didn't really believe a stone statue possessed a spirit, but I wanted to acknowledge the sculptor's spirit, which felt palpable, as well as honor the essence of the angel who inspired him.

For the next week, I spent hours every day photographing the gorgeous angel. I fell in love with her flowing hair, her crumbling hands, her cracked toes, and her delicate, upturned face. After the first few days, however, the challenge to come up with inventive angles intensified, and I felt increasingly stymied. After hours working under a blazing sun, I more or less crumpled to the ground in front of the angel and muttered under my breath how I felt fresh out of ideas, chastising myself for my limitations. After a few minutes of quiet resignation, I informed the angel that I wouldn't be returning, and, again, I whispered a prayer of thanks. While she didn't literally materialize, a cool breeze and the sudden appearance of clouds rejuvenated me.

It felt as if a presence whispered, "begin again," and, as I moved around the angel, I had difficulty keeping up with the speed at which ideas appeared. By the end of that day, I knew something magical had occurred. I bowed to the angel and left, feeling as if the statue indeed possessed a unique spirit, one that had definitely communed with my spirit.

Days later, when I began printing the film, a few images unexpectedly magnified the ethereal qualities of the angel. In one, a wispy cloud lay just behind her wings, another reflected a radiant burst of sun above her head, and another caught a minuscule white bird feather floating onto her wing. Everyone who saw the photographs thought they captured something beyond the mere physicality, which inspired me to photograph all the angels I could locate in surrounding cemeteries and museums. For the next few months, I spent so much time in the university lab printing angel photographs that my fellow photographers deemed me "the angel lady."

Although I had a successful career, photographing angels awakened something deep within, something that soon inspired me to make a huge leap of faith into a new life. The first thought occurred while photographing angels in a museum in New York. By this time, I communed with every angel I photographed, and, again, while doing so, I heard a gentle voice whisper, "follow your heart."

A few weeks later, I went to see a woman who serves as my spiritual mentor. She held some of my angel photographs in her hand and then asked me quite suddenly what I would do if I could do anything in the world. Surprisingly, the answer came immediately. "I would quit my job, fly off to Paris, and photograph angels."

Within months, stunning myself and everyone who knew me, I did exactly that. The minute I made the commitment to follow my dream, blessings occurred almost daily. Although I didn't know anyone in Paris, I found the perfect apartment and made friends instantly. While wandering the streets, cemeteries, and museums of Paris, frequently lost, not knowing where to look, I would virtually stumble upon incredible angels. I always whispered to the angels I photographed, thanking them for their beauty and promising to share their spiritual message with the world. On more than one occasion, I felt a palpable energy around me, as if someone watching over me. Frequently, at night, when I sat down to record the details of my spiritual growth, words and images flowed through my fingertips onto the page, convincing me that the angels I saw by day surrounded me at night.

On the few occasions when my spirits flagged, or when I got lost, or when self-doubt arose, I prayed to my angels. For example, after spending six hours searching fruitlessly for new angels in one of Paris' largest ancient cemeteries, a sudden thunderstorm sent me scurrying into the doorway of an open, darkened crypt. As the thunderstorm gathered and the wind increased, I pushed gently on the wrought-iron gate and inched inside. By the amount of dried leaves, branches, dirt, broken chair legs, and fragments of candelabra that littered the floor, and the thick, black cobwebs that caught in my hair, I realized that no one had set foot in this crypt for decades.

As I stood there, shivering, questioning why I had even ventured out on such a stormy day, berating myself and feeling more than a teensy bit scared, I heard a noise near the ceiling. Despite trepidation, I raised my eyes toward the ceiling and discovered four sculpted angels adorning each corner of the crypt. Although covered in black cobwebs, their alabaster forms, highly detailed wings, and chubby faces were among the most beautiful cherubs I had ever seen. I reached into my camera bag and discovered that I had one roll of film left, a type of film I rarely carried, a fast-speed film capable of capturing images in excessively dark places.

From that day forward, I felt undeniably blessed with the kind of strength, clarity, generosity, and grace that comes from feeling the presence of angels. My year in Paris was not only the culmination of a lifelong dream, but it was also a year of amazing spiritual growth. I went to Paris in search of angels; I came home feeling as if the angels of Paris had found me and, in their angelic glory, led me ever closer to my own spirit.

Susan Reynolds has been a professional writer for over twenty-five years and a photographer for fifteen years. She recently spent a year in Paris conducting extensive research and photographing angels to create her book The Angels of Paris (Les Anges de Paris), *and to record her personal journey in the form of a literary journal, entitled* Waking Up in Paris.

The Angel of Death

by Lee Beliveau

What made Charlene so special?

When I met her six months ago all I knew about her was that she was my age and was coming for a stomach test before the dialysis treatment I was scheduled to give her. She was accompanied by her mother, who like her daughter was very thin and gray-complected.

"They couldn't finish the test," Charlene told me with a smile.

My nurse's instinct warned me that she was in for a disturbing diagnosis. She would need my help, and I was happy to give it. She was very sick, having endured four failed kidney transplants, years of dialysis, and now, cancer, but she was still smiling. We were ready for each other.

On that first day, I asked her how she wanted the needles put in.

"I'm glad you asked me," she said, "how long have you been nursing in dialysis?"

She measured me up. We exchanged a few observations of the human condition, and chuckled more than once.

"I hope you're enjoying all my chatter," she confessed. "I'm usually pretty reserved—honest—it must be all the drugs they gave me in the other department."

Whatever it was, the ice was broken. Charlene impressed me with her mind, her humor, and her strength. She could handle what was coming. As a nurse and as a woman I recognized that sort of forebearance when I saw it.

"You know I have this friend who has as many medical problems as I've had," she said. "We kind of compete, in black humor. We say things like, 'Who has the biggest, darkest cloud hanging over them?' Anyway, I called her up and said, 'If this has all been a game, I win, I have cancer!'"

Over the next several months, we worked on this project together—her illness, her routines, her facing cancer. Charlene asked for the facts and she made her choices. She chose not to have treatment.

"Okay, so today I made out my will and started going though all my bookshelves," she said on Monday. "I went through the closet and dug out my size eight ball gown to give my niece. She'll love it."

On Wednesday she told me, "I'll move out of the condo and go to Mum and Dad's." To her mum she added, "and we'll get a nurse at night so you can have your sleep."

When her mum went for coffee on Thursday, Charlene confided in me. "I want them to have a party after I'm gone. I might write my own eulogy, if I have time."

When I look back on those last days of Charlene's life, I know she was guiding me on a great adventure, teaching me how to live and how to die. I enjoyed every minute with her as I tended to her needs. We talked as old friends do over a cup of tea. We had lots to chat about—her nephew's latest practical joke, her love affair, her beloved dog Buddie.

Sometimes a little symptom management thrown in on my part. We reviewed her life and her plans. I tried to put the coming loss into words for us both. "I just wish we had more time together, " I told her.

"Damn," she answered.

Charlene faced her death with relative calm. In fact, the biggest display of emotion I witnessed was were the tears of sympathy she cried when Buddie made his own trip to the animal hospital.

Charlene's courage and strength became well-known throughout our unit. Her specialist even invited her to talk to our staff about her suggestions for our unit. Charlene had become an expert, a consultant for us, and an advocate for other patients.

Before she died she left me with one last gift.

"You can always tell a good nurse by her gestures," she said.

"How did you know I was a good nurse?"

"You brought me a cold facecloth when I was retching. You noticed. You cared."

Charlene taught me that I needn't be the nurse with all the answers. I can just be a person. One who pays attention to detail. One who is unconditionally genuine. One who provides the simple gestures of caring—so profound—so clear to my patients.

"I've got so much to learn from you, I wish we'd met sooner," I told her not long before she died.

"I've often felt we've met somewhere before, do you feel that too?" She left me with one last promise. "Maybe we'll meet somewhere again."

Charlene was not just my patient; she was also my friend. I had the privilege of helping her heal before she died—and she in turn helped me accept my calling as a nurse. True to her promise, I have met her again, again, and again. I see her reflection in the eyes in every one of my patients; I hear her calm voice as I tend to them; I feel her courageous spirit fill the room when despair overcomes them. She watches over me, as I watch over them.

Lee Beliveau is a hemodialysis nurse who resides with her son, in Langley, British Columbia. Working with her dedicated colleagues and sharing the intense experiences of her patients inspires Lee to write about those scenarios in The Nephrology Nurses and Technologists Journal. *Kayaking and photography provide her with alternate glimpses of the meaning in life.*

Boomer

by Felicia Toska

*D*o guardian angels exist?

Throughout the years, I have heard from people who subscribe to religion and spirituality, and people who rebuff those beliefs and their opinions about guardian angels. Now and again I've asked people how they would describe what guardian angels are, because I never really put forth any thought as to their existence. Is a guardian angel a loved one who has passed on but is now watching over? Is a guardian angel a complete stranger who has died but has "chosen" someone to look after when needed? Does having a guardian angel mean that a higher spirit is guiding you, or does it mean a person living on earth is perhaps embodying a soul of someone who is no longer with us? Does a guardian angel even have to be a human being? I never really knew, and those with whom I've spoken gave conflicting answers, leaving me finally to ponder what a guardian angel is and, more importantly, whether I have one. Although this may appear to be somewhat unconventional, I submit that guardian angels are by nature unconventional. Aren't our guardian angels those who at impromptu moments send a warmth through our hearts, or a comfort to our damaged souls, or a calm to our minds when we need it—or even when we don't?

This certainly defies convention, where we as humans are so busy in the day-to-day grind that we do not stop to smell the roses. I know now that I do have a guardian angel. I have a presence that without my knowing, brings me peace when I have felt that giving up is easier, and even when I am just following my daily routine of living. I found my guardian angel in such a way that could only be called fate, and when I almost lost my guardian angel, I truly believed something intervened for my angel.

My angel's name is Boomer, and he is my golden retriever. I didn't believe in guardian angels before Boomer, but now I know that not only is he my guardian angel, but he has one of his own.

I can imagine the improbable eyebrow raising thoughts, but it is true, and I believe he was sent to me to look out for me. Sometimes I have imagined he is the incarnation of a gentle older woman or an innocent child who chose my Boomer because, after all, aren't our pets pure and innocent creatures who can even look at a rolled-up newspaper as a treasure?

Twelve years ago, on July 16, my former husband and I went off to purchase my first dog. I had waited all my life to get a dog, and I had imagined that my dog and I would instantly bond, much as a mother and her newborn. The puppy I was supposed to get rejected me—it whined, ran back to his mother, and was disinterested in being anywhere near me. I was heartbroken. This was an event I had waited a long time for, especially since I had problems having children of my own. My husband suggested we try another owner who had golden retriever puppies. I was sure I didn't want a golden retriever, but I felt dejected and reluctantly agreed to go. We drove to an old farmhouse in the country, and the owner advised us he had sold all the puppies but one. I sat cross-legged in the middle of the big farm kitchen, not really caring—almost like the first puppy who had no desire to see me—when a golden ball of fluff with sleepy eyes was set down in front of me. Without hesitation, he walked straight over to me, nestled in my lap, and fell asleep. That was all I needed. From then on, Boomer and I were as close as any mother and child could be.

Boomer always seemed to understand my moods. I wouldn't have to alter my behavior at all, as his cold, wet nose would bump my hand and we would sit quietly together. I felt at peace. Surprisingly, at my most melancholy times, he could be in another part of the house and suddenly appear by my side as if he sensed I needed him. I never consciously realized that he was looking out for me, however, until my first marriage broke up soon after I lost my first and only pregnancy. It was a struggle to get out of my bed each morning, but I told myself that Boomer needed me to take care of him and I didn't want to disappoint him.

What I really found out is that I needed him and his presence, and his awareness of my heartache kept me going. My Boomer looked out for me, and all the naysayers will never convince me otherwise. He saved my life, it's that simple.

Throughout the years, Boomer has been my friend, my child, my confidante, and my guardian angel.

About three months ago, Boomer suddenly collapsed in a seizure on my lap while my current husband and I were driving to drop Boomer off at my parent's home so they could "Boomer-sit."

Through my tears, I screamed at my husband to drive to the nearest veterinarian, without pausing to consider that it was eight o'clock at night. The vet's office had been closed for over an hour, but amazingly, the veterinarian had been come back to his office due to a phone call from another pet owner, and he was just preparing to leave again when we arrived.

Boomer was stabilized at the office, but the vet advised us to rush him to the emergency hospital. As we walked through the hospital doors, Boomer had another seizure in my husband's arms. I was told by Boomer's doctor that the symptoms and events appeared to indicate that he had a tumor. We had a choice to make. We could wait for confirmation by the radiologist two days later or have the vet perform surgery to determine whether this was the cause. Unfortunately, neither choice seemed destined for a positive outcome. I felt hopeless, and all Boomer did was lie on the floor next to me, where we sought comfort from one another.

Ultimately, I chose the surgical option. Hours later, I was advised that the surgical team had removed a large tumor along with Boomer's spleen, and that considering what they had found, Boomer would have died if I had chosen to wait. The timing had been crucial. My joy that he had been operated on in the nick of time was short-lived, however, as the question still remained whether the tumor was cancerous. The surgeon told me that at Boomer's age, and considering the size of the tumor, it was best that I prepare myself for the possibility that it was malignant. The common outcome was the expectation of only about a month left to live. I would know in two weeks, after the biopsy was done.

Boomer stayed in the hospital for a week, and I visited him regularly. Normally, he was a calm dog who never barked (not even if someone came to our door). The nurses told me he'd bark and bite at his cage every time I had to leave him. He wanted to come home. During my visits with him I would cry and hold him, and he looked at me with incredible intelligence and compassion, as if he were trying to comfort me.

Boomer finally came home with us, and I slept on the floor with him. When I talked to him, his tail would thump on the floor and I would just privately weep and pray that someone or something would look out for him as he had for me the past dozen years. He was an old dog, but I wasn't ready to let him go yet. I needed him.

His surgeon called on a Thursday evening the following week, and after making her repeat the results twice, I squeezed the phone with yet more tears pouring down my face. There was no cancer. The surgeon relayed that this was indeed highly unusual, and I could only smile when she said to me there must have been something looking out for him.

Boomer came out of this experience a little older, a little wobbly, and a little more tired, but those eyes—those deep, brown eyes that look right into mine—have not changed. In those eyes I see my guardian angel and I thank *his* guardian angel every day for keeping him with me just a bit longer.

Felicia Toska lives in Philadelphia with her husband, Jim; her stepchildren; Princess, their English springer spaniel; and, of course, her golden retriever, Boomer.

I Will Always Love You

by Alex Munroe

*I*t seems an eternity has passed since the story I'm about to tell changed my life, but I remember it as clearly as a summer's day. I remember warmth and promise and a powerful all-encompassing hope and desire that drives me even today, and all the days and years that follow. I find it curiously comforting to write these words, as if seeing them in print somehow makes the occurrence more permanent. A personal revelation is never easy to relate to others, for the essence of its intimacy would affect each individual differently. Of one thing, however, I am absolutely certain—for whatever universal reason, I was meant to have this encounter, and it changed my mental, physical, and spiritual life.

My tale begins more than a decade ago, when I was slogging through life in California, posing as a typical overworked urban professional. Time and tide passed through me like water, quite without my noticing its gentle flow. Enroute to the airport to begin a September vacation, I noticed the lack of color that autumn had bestowed upon the local flora. The crowded asphalt highways melted into buildings and scarred hillsides, and hardened a sky that could be cut with a knife. It was a place and time that blended into the wood-work, a place no one would ever notice.

Hours later, I was in the Midwest, preparing myself for the wedding of a very dear college friend. Not a big fan of the tra-ditional ceremony, I put on my best game face and prepared for what would be a long church service, replete with tradi-tional religious statements and taffeta concoctions adorning a host of giggly bridesmaids. After this wonderful nuptial weekend, I was free to pursue my own adventures, so I took my leave of the festivities and drove north, where I would spend the next week at a friend's family home in a charming lakeside town on Lake Michigan.

No phone, no television; just me and long strands of empty beach. I'd hoped to purge from my tired brain all thoughts of career and what little there was of a private life. After attending a wedding alone, a certain depression sets in, regardless of the circumstances. I felt the need to be cleansed from all that vexed my soul.

I went for a drive and happened upon a small rural town. I was absolutely riveted by the mass of brilliant color adorning the tree-lined streets. The red, orange, and yellow burned my eyes—such vivid color that even the best of artists could only dream of portraying. While driving down one of the main streets, I noticed an old cemetery, and given my lifelong obses-sion with all things supernatural, I couldn't help but stop.

A written description of this particular cemetery cannot give it justice, for within its confines lay stones of all sizes bordered by lush green grass and shadowed by the autumn attire of towering maples, carved into a brilliant crystal blue sky that gave them the appearance of being on fire. So beautiful was the site that I was actually taken aback—something that I rarely experienced. I was alone in this sacred place, and as always, I took great care not to step where I shouldn't and to pay my own respects to those whose refuge this place represented. I meandered slowly from one stone to the next, trying to imagine the lives these individuals had once led. They were people just like us—men, women, children, soldiers, wives, mothers, grandparents—who left their mark on this world, and I was bearing witness to their final tribute. It was, and always shall be, an honor to read the names and words upon these stones and of all those who once stood on solid ground.

I wondered how these people had survived in life. Were they happy or sad? Did they merely survive, or did they have good fortune in life? Had they ever found true love? Had they suffered through personal triumph or tragedy? Was death a relief or the ultimate torment? So many questions unanswered, so many different lives and different circumstances. When asking such queries of others, one can't help but direct those questions inward. Was I really happy? What had I accomplished in my life? Would I ever find my true love? Odd as it may sound, I've always felt a certain comfort in the resting places of those who have passed on. The sense of peace is something I craved, and these places are without turmoil and extraneous distraction. It is a place of whispers and silent wandering. For a short while, I rested under the shade of a gnarled maple, a blanket of fallen leaves padding the smooth roots that had pushed through the musty earth. I felt an emptiness amid the silence, an emptiness that I cannot attribute specifically to loneliness, or despair, or hopelessness. I suppose it was a combination of everything, such as humans often experience but are loathe to admit. I had done so much with my life, or so I'd thought, but there was so much that was lost in the gray reality of the daily existence that consumed me. I was the gray speck surrounded by the fiery flames of autumn. I was unnoticeable.

In time, I continued my stroll and came upon a small clearing. For whatever reason, I stopped for a moment, and a sharp breeze blew across my face, pushing my hair over my shoulder. I looked up and listened, but there was no sound to be heard. There wasn't the slightest breeze moving through the trees overhead or through the grasses covering the grounds. Unable to move, I stood still and silent, waiting to feel the cool air of another aberrant breeze. It came. Only this time it was stronger, and in a voice as clear as rain I heard the words: "I will always love you."

The hair on my neck stood on end as I immediately swirled around, scanning the cemetery for the source of the voice. I was alone and the trees were as still as stone.

Of what happened next, I can say simply this: I know only that which I see and hear to be true. Nothing more, nothing less. I was moved to turn in a certain direction, and I started walking toward a headstone that lay crookedly in the distance. I came upon the small monolith from behind and moved to face it head on.

Etched upon the stone was a simple phrase, and my heart stopped when I gazed upon it. In clear letters, it read: *I Will Always Love You.* Nothing more. Nothing less.

A decade has passed since I wandered that beautiful place on a warm autumn afternoon. Unlike the many other places I've seen in my travels, that wonderful old cemetery was a gift. After arriving home from that trip, I ended my job, moved away, and began an adventure of life more suited to my passions. Along the way I met my true love. The loneliness, despair, and hopelessness that overcame me that day at the cemetery has given way to has compassion, companionship, and hope. The gray area of my existence is now awash with color, its faded facade now bedecked with tiles of peace and acceptance.

The angel who spoke to me was indeed watching over me, and probably has been for a very long time. As the circle of my life continues on its path, I know I can count on my guardian angel's divine intervention when I need it.

Alex Munroe is a graphic designer and self-proclaimed adventurer of humanity. Based in Oregon, she spends the majority of her time glued to her computer. The irresistible lure of exploring old cemeteries continues to this day.

Strength of an Angel

by Kathy Easson

*T*he normal life of an eleven-year-old child usually doesn't involve many shocking experiences. In 1958, I was growing up in the transient lifestyle of a military family, where the usual surprise was being informed that my father was being transferred and we were moving again. It was certainly not an event that required angelic intervention, and for our family, it was not an unexpected event. Relocating had become commonplace, and even at that tender age, I was a seasoned traveler, having lived in Utah, Michigan, Kansas, and the Philippines, where I learned my first words in Tagalog, at the feet of a Filipino housekeeper.

My father was an Air Force officer—a pilot drawn to that branch of the military by his passion for flying and obsession with mechanical contraptions. In the first years of his career, Dad had developed a close friendship with a fellow officer who had a sister that he thought Dad would be interested in meeting. Boy, was he ever right. Sparks flew, and just a few weeks after introductions were made, my parents were married in the Presbyterian church in my mother's hometown.

Nine months (and a few hours) later, I became their first child—a daughter—with a brother and sister to follow just a few years later.

During my earliest years, my father was kept busy flying missions to faraway lands. My first memories are of him in his crisp blue uniform, replete with shiny buttons, medals, and colorful ribbons. Dad was larger than life and seemed, at times, almost divine. If angels existed, I thought, they probably looked like my father. Little did I know at the time that my father and I would eventually have our own encounter with a true guardian angel.

Our recent relocation in 1958 had brought us to Lake Charles, a Louisiana bayou city steeped in French Acadian influences. After long discussions, my parents decided to set down roots, primarily to give me and my younger brother and sister a sense of permanence. They purchased a small house on a one-acre lot on the outskirts of town, converted the garage into a master bedroom, and for the first time in my life, we called our living quarters "home."

Living miles away from the Air Force Base in an intensely Southern community was a brand-new experience for my siblings and me. Mysterious and melodious Cajun and Creole dialects floated throughout the marketplaces and cafeterias, and we found new friends in the neighborhood with fascinating surnames that rolled off your tongue, like Gaspar, Prudhomme, and Boudreaux.

Even in those relatively modern times, the Civil War was still a painful thorn that would elicit passionate debate and resentment among our youthful peers. With the flexibility of youth, we quickly integrated ourselves into life in the deep South, adopting a passable Southern *patois*, and vigorously belittling anyone suspected of being a much-despised Yankee. Even after forty-four years, when I find myself conversing with a native Southerner, I still subconsciously slip into a drawl that will "y'all" you to death.

Our parents viewed our transformation with bemusement and understanding—along with a steady hand on the reins and a strong Christian influence. We were taught to take our new surroundings in historical and cultural context. Nowhere would this be more influential on our lives than in dealing with the racism, segregation, and attitudes that so completely skewed the thinking of many Southern adolescents.

One day, my brother, who was nine at the time, rather stupidly made a comment about African-Americans, using the worst pejorative term possible. My father, home on one of his leaves of duty, hauled him up short.

"Where did you hear that word?" my father asked.

"My friends say it all the time," said my brother, wide-eyed and startled.

My father glared at him and said, "You need to understand that your friends are part of their environment and upbringing. That upbringing is based on intolerance and ignorance, and I will not have ignorance in this house!"

Dad was dead serious. I knew it, and my brother, who was the recipient of this reaction and the no-nonsense cultural lesson that followed, most certainly knew it. Having been brought up by intelligent and tolerant parents, we had been relatively sealed off from the realities of segregation and racism. In the late 1950s, in our new home in Lake Charles, these issues were essentially a fact of life. My father explained in great detail how this was ethically and intellectually wrong, and although there was little we could do to change the viewpoints of our peers, we should never let the ignorance of others affect our own opinions.

I had been troubled by the racial attitudes of my own friends and their families, but my father's careful explanations verified my own forming opinions and helped me come to terms with a life that I was learning to love—only now with a healthy distrust of prejudice. I had never admired my father more.

Not long after this incident, my father made time to work on the family car that my mother had recently purchased, a huge 1958 Oldsmobile sedan. As my father recalls, a few bolts had worked loose under the front end of the vehicle.

With his mechanical experience and independent nature, Dad saw no point in taking the car to the dealership. Instead, he jacked up the front end of the car, removed the wheels, and busied himself with what he considered to be minor repairs.

My brother and sister were off playing with friends while Mom and I remained in the house doing chores. To this day, I can't explain it, but out of the blue I was suddenly overwhelmed with fear. I knew something was horribly wrong. I raced outside and into the driveway. I saw the car resting on the wheel hubs, virtually flat on the ground, and I could hear my father struggling to breathe.

Screaming in panic, I grabbed the bumper of the car and lifted. The next thing I remember is my father's voice, whispering in my ear—a calm, soothing voice that quelled all other worldly sound.

"It's okay, Kathy, you can let it down," he said. I didn't believe him, and refused to let go.

"It's okay," he said. "Let it down. I'm right here." Only then did I realize that my father was there beside me. I let go of the bumper, gasping and crying in relief.

As my father recounts the story, he had assumed that the repair work would take only a few minutes; he hadn't bothered to put supporting jack stands in place after he'd raised the front end and removed the wheels, instead relying on the bumper jack to hold the car (a mistake he would never make again). Moments after he had slid beneath the vehicle, the bumper jack slipped and the car crashed down on him. As fortune would have it, he was lying with his head in the only clear area in the car's undercarriage, but the weight of the car was on the wheel hubs, and on his chest. He knew he was in serious trouble and was slowly being crushed. Suddenly, he felt the weight rise off his chest, and with inches to spare, he shoved himself to freedom, only to find his 11-year-old daughter holding up the front end of a two-ton car. As he put it, "I had to do some coaxing to get you to set the car back down."

Dad had bruises on his chest that lasted for weeks. My physical side effects were nonexistent. No pulled muscles, no back pain—nothing. The important side effect is that my father is still alive, still happy, and still with me. I imagine that everyone has heard stories of adrenaline-pumped feats of superhuman strength, and I don't really doubt any of them. I'm absolutely certain, as is my father, that no amount of adrenaline could produce enough strength in a stick-thin sixty-pound kid to pick up the front end of an Oldsmobile.

Was this the work of my guardian angel? Of my father's, perhaps? I really can't say for certain. But I do know, and will always be certain of the fact, that I didn't do it by myself. Whatever guardian angel visited us on that day, in that place and time, knew the value of my father and his insights into all that is good about the human spirit.

Kathy Easson and her husband, Alan, live and work in Hollywood, California. A longtime associate with the Church of Scientology, Kathy has devoted her life to helping others.

Heaven on Earth

by Eric Mochnacz

I've always believed in God, and I've always believed that He lets things happen for a reason. I also believe that He puts people in our lives to watch over us and care for us and lift us up—His angels on earth. I believe that God has given me angels on earth.

When my my brother Jay died at the age of twenty-two, my belief in God and His angels was tested. On May 31, 2001, my mother found Jay lying dead at the bottom of our basement stairs. He had been living in the basement with the goal of renovating it so that he and I could have our own rooms. Sometime during the night, he had fallen backward down the stairs and cracked his skull on the concrete floor.

I was eighteen at the time, and I remember walking through that day in a daze—numb to everything. We had two wakes, and both of them had a line of mourners out the door. Jay had left such a legacy that people he hadn't spoken with in five years were there to pay their final respects. People who had never even met Jay but were my friends, or friends of my sister's, came to help us through our tough time, knowing how important he was to our lives.

At the wake my young cousin Tyler took my hand and said, "I want to pray for Jay now."

He led me to the coffin so I could pray with him, and as I knelt, I knew that at that moment, Tyler was one of my angels. During a tumultuous time, he was letting me know, in small measure, that my brother would be all right.

Life went on for the most part, but I missed my brother, and worried about him. Unlike me, Jay was not a religious person, and we had argued often about the existence of God. If Jay did not believe in God, as he sometimes claimed, was he in heaven?

Some nights, I'd be driving home from youth group, pass by my local church, and just cry because I missed Jay so much. I would go to prayer nights and they would play a song called "Remember Me," and I would bawl as my friends held me. Again, those people who comforted me and wiped away my tears were God's angels on earth.

Several months later, in July 2001, I went to my second Steubenville East Conference. Steubenville is a Catholic youth conference organized by the Franciscan University of Steubenville in Ohio. The group had branched out to all parts of the nation, and we went to an event held in Attleboro, Massachusetts.

When my brother died, I didn't exactly lose faith in God, but I felt numb. I didn't really try to live my faith as I had tried before. I didn't put a lot of effort into anything. I felt empty inside. One of the Steubenville traditions is that on Saturday night they have "Adoration of the Blessed Sacrament." During this event, a representation of Jesus is displayed in the form of the Eucharist, and everyone in the crowd is encouraged to pray and really let Jesus work in their lives. So, I knelt and I prayed, but I felt such an overwhelming sadness as the priest carried Jesus around, displaying Him for everyone to see, that I began to bawl. All I could feel was God and me—one and one—and all the sadness I had harbored since Jay's death. It was palpable. I could feel it.

At these types of events, it is common practice for people to pray over each other. Because I was attending with my youth group, I knew many of my fellow worshippers. These same individuals had been the ones to comfort me during Jay's death. As they comforted me again now, I remembered how my brother and I had argued about God. Some days he would say he didn't even believe in Him just to get on my nerves. My brother didn't go to Mass and didn't really ascribe to any religion, though he had researched many different religions. He even had books in our room about Wicca. Where religion was concerned, we were polar opposites. I was the Jesus freak and Jay was...just Jay.

I prayed for him, and remembered what Tyler had said at Jay's wake. I was obviously hoping that Jay was in heaven, but at the same time, why would God accept him into eternity if Jay had said he didn't even believe in Him? Could he really be in heaven? Or did God turn him away as he may have turned away from God?

It was at that moment that God sent me another guardian angel. At that very moment of spiritual questioning, my youth minister, Chrissy, knelt down beside me—a simple action that still brings on tears. She put her arm lightly on my back and said, "Eric, I don't know why God is having me say this, but you need to know that Jay is in heaven with Him."

I broke down. I cried so much that night, out of both sadness and relief, but after all the tears, I was allowed to smile with joy in my heart because of what God's angel had said to me that night. Jay was in heaven and he was at peace. My cousin Tyler had started me on this journey of awareness and acceptance, and now Chrissy had completed the circle. Both of these wonderful individuals were watching out for me with their divine intervention, and I will forever be thankful for their presence.

Eric Mochnacz is twenty-one and a communications major at Seton Hall University. He works as a resident assistant and plans to pursue a career in that field.

Miracle on the Mangala Express

by Erin Reese

$\mathcal{N}$orthern India was freezing. In the midst of the country's most brutal winter in forty years, the region had turned into one giant Popsicle. I was studying yoga in Rishikesh, at the base of the Himalayas in mid-January, and I could no longer lift my stiff, frozen joints out of bed. The savage cold showed no signs of letting up, so my new travel buddy, Katy, and I admitted defeat. Saying good-bye to our icy guesthouse, we set out for the warmer climes of the southern state of Karnataka, where coconut groves, balmy breezes, and bathtub-temperature ocean waters awaited us.

After three weeks of navigating through a jungle of red tape, we finally secured our reservations for the grueling three-day journey. We would have to take an overnight train from Rishikesh to Old Delhi Station, and with a little more than two hours to spare, catch a cab to Nizamuddin Station on the other side of New Delhi, climb aboard the Mangala Lakshadweep Express, and head south.

As the overnight train sputtered toward Delhi, I cowered in my upper berth after a cold sleepless night. Are we even going anywhere? I thought I'd never seen a train move so slowly. All night long, and into the wee hours of the morning, our train would lurch forward, screech to a halt, trudge off a little further, and stop again.

My heart began to sink as our scheduled time of arrival came and went. This is India, not Europe, I reminded myself. An Indian train arrives in her own sweet time.

As our train lolled along, I sank deeper into my doldrums and glanced over at my travel mate, Katy, peering peacefully out the window on her side of the compartment. How could she look so untroubled when we were going to be stranded in the congested, polluted, freezing armpit of "Smelly Delhi," with no chance of getting another train south in this holiday mess? Katy, with her rosy cheeks and untroubled smile, was a free-spirited traveling sprite, ten years my junior. As we waited on the train platform the night before, she had busied herself by sorting through her rucksack contents. After spilling out assorted piles of hippie beads, musical instruments, and batik tapestries, Katy finally unearthed a small bag of treasures.

"What is that?" I asked, pointing to a tiny wooden box wrapped in a scrap of velvet.

"Oh, that's my guardian angel," Katy replied cheerily. She opened the box and handed me the miniature figurine. "A friend gave her to me before I left England.

"She said if I ever need help out of a jam, I should just call upon this little angel and she'll help me out!"

Amused, I looked at the cheap gold plastic angel pin in my palm. Isn't that sweet, I thought wryly. What some people put their faith in!

Back on the "Slow Poke Express," the minutes ticked by— we were two hours late, and we were about to be stranded in a remote section of Delhi with no recognizable landmarks, lost in a sea of foreign faces. I began to panic. As our train approached the station, Katy and I grabbed our packs and bolted for the door. We didn't have a second to spare if we wanted half a chance to make our connecting train on the other side of Delhi.

"No Madame! Danger!" yelled an elderly Indian in a white Gandhi tunic. Ignoring his warning, I leapt off the side of the slowing train. I tumbled down onto the hard cement platform and collapsed under the weight of my backpack.

Thanking the heavens above that I hadn't sprained my ankle, I scrambled after Katy toward the station exit.

"You want rickshaw? You are wanting a ride? I make you good price! Best price!" Squeezing past the tidal wave of rickshaw wallahs, we made our way for the taxi queue. Just up ahead, we spotted a lone driver who was smoking a bidi next to his white minicab, bouncing up and down to stay warm. This was a feat for nothing less than deities. In order to catch our connecting train at Nizamuddin Station, we needed our cab—our chariot—to sprout wings and catapult us all the way across India's sprawling, congested capital city in just twenty minutes.

"Go!" we shouted, as our driver floored it, squealing out of the lot, with the little lawnmower-size engine screeching in protest. Not too far from our departure point, we sat barricaded in the biggest traffic jam I'd ever seen—incessant horn honking, crammed motor scooters, auto rickshaws, delivery trucks, and taxis—for a solid ten minutes.

Trapped in an unmoving cab, I had less faith than a mustard seed has that we would ever catch our train. The culprit of our gridlock was the most sacred creature in India: a holy cow. No one would dare disrupt the milking cow's path as she took her own sweet time ambling across the sprawling intersection.

Feeling desperate, I glanced at the blinking, lighted altar of the pot-bellied, elephant-headed god Ganesh, perched on the cab's dashboard. Sitting in a plume of incense smoke, the jolly deity appeared to be smiling at me. I closed my eyes, took a deep breath, and inhaled a big dose of "Eau de Parfum d'India," a potpourri of excrement, diesel exhaust, and temple incense.

Okay, Ganesh, I silently pleaded. You're the Divine Remover of Obstacles, right? So, show me your stuff and start by removing this divine cow from our path!

Awestruck, I watched as the divine bovine slowly but surely sauntered to the side of the road. Like the parting of the Red Sea, the sacred animal had left a swath of empty road in her wake. Our driver seized the opportunity to be the hero of the day, expertly maneuvering the cab into the cleared path.

He gunned the engine, plowed through the intersection, and sped us off toward Nizamuddin Station just as fast as the hiccuping cab could go. Just one block before our departure station, we found ourselves trapped in yet another unyielding traffic jam. In his thick Indian accent, our driver commanded us: "You are now having to get out and run! You are only having four minutes to catch train!"

I shoved 300 rupee notes at him, and Katy and I bolted for the station.

We were two crazed, disheveled white women with over-stuffed backpacks, panicked eyes, and bed-head hair flying everywhere. Determined to make that train, I breathlessly wheezed out at the top of my tired lungs, "Somebody help us!!! We need a porter!"

We had absolutely no idea which platform our train, the Mangala Lakshadweep Express, would be departing from. All signs and systems were posted in Hindi, without a word of English to be seen anywhere.

With less than thirty seconds to spare, I decided to take my chances. I wished I had a guardian angel in my pocket. But maybe Katy's would do. Running full force, I picked a random track and flew down the steps toward the train, praying it was the right one. Sweaty, dirty, and desperate, I could barely eke out the name of our train as I bellowed, "Is this the Mangala Express?"

The answer, thank God, was yes. We flung ourselves onboard as the train instantly began moving beneath our feet. Still smiling beatifically, Katy led the way to our reserved compartment. Panting, with burning, tired lungs, I struggled to follow her. "I cannot believe we made it, Katy! I just did NOT think it was possible! How did that happen?!"

"Oh, I knew we'd make it," chirped Katy. "I told you, I have a guardian angel, and you, my friend, obviously have one, too!"

As our train lumbered toward the warm, tropical south of India, I stood unmoving, gazing out the window for a long time. I was not one of the millions of spiritual seekers who pour into this ancient, sacred land every year in search of enlightenment. I made fun of these tourists and their so-called gurus, as I laughed at the cab driver's Ganesh and Katy's guardian angel. But I wasn't laughing any more. In a place where miracles were seen as everyday events, I myself had experienced a miracle of sorts. I'd have to get myself one of Katy's little guardian angels. In the meantime, I offered up a big prayer of gratitude to the guardian angel who performed the Miracle of the Mangala Express.

Erin Reese is a globe-trotting writer, speaker, and visionary. In between backpacking journeys to faraway lands, Erin works as a corporate recruiter in San Francisco and New York City.

Angels Do Lunch

by Paula Munier

When I was a little girl, my mother told me that my guardian angel was there watching over me at all times. And she offered proof of my guardian angel's existence: Whenever I disobeyed her, and then managed to trip over my own two feet, my mother would say, "Your guardian angel did that to you!" Thereby proving that my guardian angel was right there, monitoring my every move and making sure that I was a good girl and did the right thing, particularly when it came to my mother. This inevitably became a self-fulfilling prophecy; whenever I displeased my mother, I would invariably fall on my face. (Thanks to my hypervigilant spy from heaven, I developed a well-deserved reputation as a klutz, which continues to this day.)

"Your guardian angel did that to you." Lest I think of my guardian angel as merely a disciplinarian, my mother would always add, "She's there whenever you need her, to protect you, to keep you safe, and to help you be your best self. All you have to do is ask."

Despite this disclaimer, I mostly thought of my guardian angel as a pain in the butt, just one more grown-up telling me what to do—until I started school. My father was in the military, and we moved at least once a year. This had little effect on my early childhood, when all I needed was my parents and some playmates to share the sandbox, but once I started school, the pressure was on to win friends and influence people—from my teachers to my peers. I was always the new kid. I usually showed up at my new school in the middle of the year, when all the other kids there had already made their friends and settled into the little cliques that arise in such a setting. Making friends in a new school is never easy, and doing it in the middle of the year is the hardest thing of all.

The first day was predictably torturous. It didn't matter what kind of school it was—military, public, Catholic, American, or foreign. It didn't matter where the school was—Oklahoma, Germany, Georgia, or Kansas. I was the new kid, and so the scenario was always the same. Year after year, school after school—twelve schools in eleven years—I suffered through that terrible first day as if I were caught in continuous replay, my own movie version of *Groundhog Day*.

I could never sleep the night before a first day at a new school, so I would wake up tired and grouchy and scared. I dressed very carefully, never knowing how the kids in this particular part of the world dressed, and always got it wrong.

My mother would give me the usual pep talk in the car on the way. *Isn't this fun, going new places, meeting new people. Think of all the new things you'll learn, and the new friends you'll make. You're going to love it here.* Outside the school, she'd stop, lean down, and take me by the shoulders. She'd look right into my eyes and say, "There's nothing to be afraid of. They're going to love you. If you get scared, just ask your guardian angel for help." Then my mother would take me to the principal's office, where she'd present my yellow shot records and faded birth certificate, fill out the paperwork, smile that glorious smile of hers, and then abandon me to the school secretary.

The school secretary would then march me down the hallway to hell—my new classroom. She would hand me over like a lost kitten, and I'd stand there at the front of the room, by the teacher's desk. The teacher would say, "Class, this is our new student." She'd pause to read my name off my paperwork—Paula Sue Munier—forget any French she'd ever known, and say: "Paula Sue Manure."

All the children would laugh, and then that smart-aleck boy at the back of the room—there's always a smart-aleck boy at the back of the room—would yell out: "Pile of Sewer Manure, Pile of Sewer Manure!"

The kids would howl, and order in the classroom would take days to restore. I would turn every shade of red and want to turn and run back home into my mother's arms. But I never did. I stood there, head held high, eyes straight ahead, and I endured, and I never cried, no matter how hard the kids laughed, because I knew that this was not the worst of it.

The worst moment always came later, at lunchtime. Lunchtime strikes fear in the heart of every new kid at school. Being called a pile of sewer manure was nothing compared to the potential humiliation of eating alone—an outcast in a sea of screaming kids stuffing cafeteria-style pizza and creamed corn down their throats.

I'd line up with the rest of the kids, my lunch ticket clasped in my sweaty little hand. I'd take a tray and give the cafeteria lady my ticket, and then face what remains for me the most terrifying prospect on Planet Earth: a lunchroom full of strangers.

This was always when my courage would fail me. I'd stand there, head bowed, defeated, all alone, while my peers streamed around me, laughing, talking, hanging out together. I never knew what to do. The thought of making that long walk alone down through the long tables, armed with kids who didn't know who I was and, more important, didn't care, was simply too awful. So I would just stand there. A lonely, scared little girl in a big, lonely place full of people, an impulse away from crying for my mother. That's when I'd remember what she'd told me that morning in front of the school building. *If you get scared, just ask your guardian angel for help.* My hands would tighten around my tray, and I'd pray. "Please, Guardian Angel, don't let me eat lunch alone. Send me a friend."

At this very moment, year after year, school after school, first day after first day, an angel would appear at my side. An earth angel, in the form of a kid just like me, who knew how terrible it must be to eat alone in the lunchroom.

"Want to eat with us?"

I was saved! I would thank my guardian angel under my breath, and then happily follow my new best friend to a table full of other new best friends, and get on with the serious business of being a kid.

To this day, I have a soft spot in my heart for those kind souls who asked me to lunch on those dreadful first days of school. I'm in my late forties now, and I still suffer a momentary panic every time I have to enter a room full of strangers. But I know that no matter what else happens, I'll never have to eat lunch alone. As my mother would say, "Your guardian angel did that to you."

Paula Munier (pronounced munYAY) is a writer and editor. The mother of three, she lives in Salem, Massachusetts. She is still a klutz.

Riding with an Angel

by Anne Maxwell

*N*ow you'll always have a guardian angel watching over you," someone told me after my mother died seven years ago. I dismissed that as sentimental hogwash, the sort of thing you say when you don't know what else to say. It took a ride on a Harley to convince me otherwise.

My mother and father's only mode of transportation after they were married was his motorcycle, a 1937 Harley-Davidson Panhead—a bike he was sadly compelled to part with when he left to serve our country when we entered World War II. While I was growing up, I remember Mom talking fondly of those first years, and I loved looking at the few photographs of them dressed in the riding attire of their day: bomber jackets, flight boots, leather helmets, and woolen scarves.

My own first experience on a Harley was with my dad when I was a teenager in the sixties. Dad had decided it was time to get back into the world of motorcycles, and he treated himself to a 1966 Harley-Davidson Electra

Glide. He rode that bike to work virtually every day. Although I loved the sound of the engine starting up in the morning as I was getting ready for school, I was afraid of actually riding on the bike. Mom assured me that my father was always careful and would be extra cautious with me on board. With that in mind, I asked Dad for a ride, and on weekends we would roar off, with me holding on to him for dear life, my terror lightened only by the pure joy of being behind my father on his Harley, sharing Mom's faith.

Many years later, my husband, Bob, expressed a deep admiration for Harleys. Shortly after my mother's passing it became obvious to me that he really did want to own one. I still had a healthy fear of motorcycling, and I had heard about and seen horrible accidents involving motorcyclists. Then I thought about my parents, and remembered the enjoyment they had shared during their riding days. I was sure I was crazy, but I sensed Mom's presence. I could feel her confidence, and knowing she would be our guardian angel, I supported my husband in finding just the right bike.

Soon there was a gleaming Harley-Davidson sitting in our garage. As soon as Bob was comfortable handling the machine, I became his passenger. As I sat nervously behind him for our first ride together, thoughts of my mother came into my mind, and I felt my guardian angel was with me.

We found ourselves taking day outings, which soon turned into overnight trips, then weeklong jaunts, and ultimately, longer riding vacations. It was during all of those trips and all of those miles that I recognized what a truly bonding experience our Harley-Davidson had become for us. Not only had I learned how to place absolute trust in my husband while being his passenger, but we were also developing an expanded relationship as a result of our planning, absorbing new scenery together, and sharing conversations with the ever-present Harley admirers.

It was also during those trips that I began recognizing that Dad's genes were running strongly through me. I wanted to experience the sensation of being the operator of a Harley-Davidson. Bob supported me, just as I had supported him, and soon there was a beautiful 2000 Fat Boy parked in our garage next to his bike. I started out tentatively, following Bob's lead, and quickly discovered the true joy of being in control of my own motorcycle. After the initial break-in period of my bike, it wasn't long before we were back in the groove of exploring uncharted country on two bikes. We found that riding next to one another brought us even closer. A newfound trust and confidence was being developed as we learned to ride together, whether he was in the lead, I was in the lead, or we were riding next to one another.

After racking up 60,000 miles on his Road King, Bob made the decision to turn it in for a brand-new 2003 Screaming Eagle Road King. That decision found us once again going through the break-in process of a new motorcycle.

Living on the Oregon coast as we do, we decided the perfect break-in ride would be to a favorite spot in the south, along the Oregon coastal highway. We started out on a beautiful sunny, brisk morning. We made a few stops as we rode, taking our time and stopping to admire the scenery along the way. As the day wore on, we found we needed one last stop before arriving at our destination.

We pulled into a rest stop just outside of Brookings for a few relaxing minutes, and then we were off . . . or so we thought. For the first time on one of our trips, my Fat Boy had developed a mechanical problem and wouldn't start. We tried all the tricks to get it going, but ultimately realized we needed help. A cell phone call soon brought a tow truck to us.

The driver was a friendly young man, and we made arrangements to meet him and my bike the next day at the nearest dealership.

Once again I found myself saddling up behind my husband. As we left the rest area, the sun was just setting over the Pacific Ocean and, as a passenger, I was able to savor every moment of watching it disappear into the horizon in all of its spectacular color. We soon turned on to Highway 199, making our way through majestic redwood groves to our special getaway, Patrick Creek Lodge.

The next morning we woke to temperatures in the low thirties and climbed aboard Bob's motorcycle for the trip to meet my disabled Fat Boy. The ride took us along the Smith River, with its breathtaking views and breathtaking curves. I found I only had to close my eyes two or three times as we rounded some of those curves with logging trucks rushing at us. But that's when it hit me.

There we were, riding one motorcycle together, just like in the beginning of our riding days, just like my mother and father had ridden sixty years ago. I allowed myself to relax and place my trust in my husband. The day turned into one of the most gratifying of our marriage for both of us. I was riding with him again, but it was even more special, as we rode his brand-new bike together. I would never have ridden behind him if my motorcycle had not broken down. Fate? Who knows. I do know that my mother is with us every time we ride. And on that special day, I felt her with me, my guardian angel, keeping us safe, proudly riding through me behind her own beloved husband.

Anne Maxwell is the mother of two wonderful children, Mariah and Dustin. Avid motorcyclists, Anne and her husband Bob live, work, and play on Oregon's central coast.

Martha

by Geralynn Spann Smith
as told by Tammy Dill Rust

My father, Graham Dill, had a signature sign-off for me with every written e-mail, spoken voice-mail, and conversation. He would always close by stating calmly, "Remember, God loves you, and so do I."

On April 29, 2000, while I was visiting my dear father during the Easter holiday, he suddenly died. Death always spurs symptoms of sadness and despair to the living spirit, but in my case, the grief was particularly deep. I had always been quite close to my father, and his absence left a massive void in my heart. At once, the shining sun had lost much of its luminance.

After returning to Delaware for the funeral, I visited my adopted teen son, Robert, to deliver the bad news. Robert was a resident of the Sussex County (DE) Work Release Program due to a recurring substance abuse problem. He was also very close to his grandfather, whom he affectionately knew as "Pop."

Through the most difficult times, Dad would support Robert as he battled the demons of vice and addiction. He was an inspiration and a pillar of love for Robert to lean against, so the news was devastating and not well received.

Three days later, I reluctantly returned to work, teaching at the local elementary school, depressed but determined to move forward and stay positive. As a Christian woman in the Episcopal Church, I believed God would be there for me, no matter what the condition or circumstance. As I would soon come to realize, God never promised that no sorrow would fall upon His children, only that He would be there to comfort us and share in the pain.

The following morning the phone rang. It was Robert's natural aunt with more bad news. Robert's birth mother had passed away. The aunt asked me to inform Robert. I dreaded again being the bearer of ill tidings, and prayed for strength. I knew in advance the visit would be one of the most difficult, toughest chores I would ever have to complete in my entire life, but it had to be done.

Two sleepless days later, I again visited my only son, nervous and saddened. Robert's counselor joined us as we sat together around a small table in a colorless room. Above, fluorescent lighting hummed mournfully.

As expected, the news did not fall on happy ears. At first, Robert said nothing, deep in private thought, emotions roiling within, like a storm gathering strength. Then, he stood up, stared deep into my face with tearful eyes, and without warning, slammed his chair violently into the table. He ran from the room, engulfed in grief. Although he hadn't spoken a word, his actions spoke volumes.

I was numb with pain, and my heart seemed to split within my chest. So often the messenger bears the brunt of the recipient's emotions when the news is bad. It's not a matter of fairness but, rather, one of convenience. The counselor rose and left without a word, leaving me alone. Several minutes later I exited the silent room, feeling utterly hopeless and emotionally drained. I felt the urge to get sick, to crawl into a vacant corner somewhere far away, curl into a quaking ball of frayed feelings, and die. The pain of my father's passing was still very much present, crushing, and something I was still coming to terms with. Now I felt rejected by my beloved child, at a time when I wanted to help him cope with news that was understandably upsetting. It was also a time when I needed him.

I drifted out of the building and across the parking lot to my car, like a vanquished spirit oblivious of everything around me. Somehow I got into my car before sobs for help exploded across my steering column and dashboard. I sat there for several minutes, crying and shaking, out of control, never feeling more alone in my life than at this moment. Then, a knocking on the window of my car door startled me. Partly embarrassed and a little annoyed at the intrusion, I glanced up through swollen, red eyes to view the uninvited visitor. Standing at the side of my car was an African American woman with a kind face and tender eyes that were gentle and bright. She motioned for me to roll down my window, and I obeyed. The lady smiled and introduced herself simply as Martha.

Martha said softly, "I don't know who you are, but God spoke to my heart to come over to you."

I couldn't speak, so I listened intently, and with an expectant heart.

"I don't know what is going on in your life right now, but be assured that things will get better."

Then, without hesitation, Martha leaned down closer and into the car to hug me. She whispered into my ear, "Remember, God loves you, and so do I."

I crumbled, having heard the exact words my wonderful father shared with me on every occasion, but now voiced by a total stranger.

By the time I had regained my composure, Martha was gone. I looked everywhere, but the woman had literally disappeared. I would never see her ever again, at the center, around town, anywhere.

Did an angel visit me that day, sent from God above, at a crucial time of need? Could it have been the spirit of my father, working through this kind earthly soul of a woman, sending me the message that I wasn't alone, and that I would never be alone? Regardless, the message of the event rings true: "Love one another as I have loved you."

Or, in the case of my father, Graham Dill, "Remember, God loves you, and so do I."

Geralynn Spann Smith works full-time as a senior application support specialist for Delaware's Department of Transportation. She loves reading and cooking and dreams of one day opening "Geri's Cafe," a bookstore/coffee shop. She and her husband, David, plan to adopt a baby girl from China in the fall of 2004.

Seals

by Eydith Johnson

Ever since I was young, I have suffered from insomnia. As a child in my bed, I saw visions of darkness. Once, while in bed looking out into the lavender walls in the hallway, I saw the walls turn red. I put my head under the covers and felt the presence of someone standing over me. It was a dark shadow. I told the devil to go away, and then I prayed for good dreams to come my way.

I was a sickly child. No one liked me in school and everyone said I'd never succeed in life, just have a lot of babies. I always wrote poems, but my family said I'd need to get a real job and stop dreaming. The Lord kept a pen in my hand, and for that reason I wrote poetry and only had two children. I learned nothing is free except prayer, and I am inspired by people who get off their butts and work.

I was raised in church and remember holding hands in prayer with my eyes closed. I would get brightness in vision while holding hands with perfect strangers. I would sweat, and it felt as if I were being lifted off the floor. I don't think I was, but it sure felt like it. This meant to me that the Lord was hearing my prayers.

That's why he sent me Seals, my angel on earth. Seals was a nice man I met when a so-called boyfriend left me, and I was at a club, depressed. He came over to me and bought me a drink. He danced with me, and we talked. We ended up spending a lot of time together. Seals was the first man to take me anywhere and not want sex. He was blessed in the Lord and we spoke about the Lord often.

Seals was in a bad marriage. At the time I didn't understand why people stayed in bad marriages when they weren't happy.

Seals was a drinker. He killed his liver, and he knew he was going to die. He always said, "God willing we will be together, but nothing is promised."

No one could believe it, reading the obituary, that my friend had died. We'd spoken just the night before, and he hadn't mentioned being ill. The next day he died. I cried all day and all night. Seals had brought happiness into my life. I wrote a poem about him when he died:

SEALS
Your angel came to lift you high,
you're flying now, you're in the sky,
I never got to say good-bye.
Here's to you, Seals fly high.
We plant a seed and watch it grow,
We dream a dream until no more.
Our time on earth has no date,
until the Lord picks up His slate.

Had he not died, I'm sure I would have married him. Instead I married someone else. My husband was the devil.

He drank, and heard me talking about him, and choked me as I slept. He took my diamonds, my change; he took the grandbabies' money. I never received anniversary, Christmas, or birthday gifts. He decided he wasn't going to celebrate. I couldn't breathe in my marriage. I couldn't sleep. I lived with this man for seven years and tried to make it work because I believed the Lord wanted me to see what a bad man really was before I decided to do it again.

I always believed the Lord kept me in that relationship as a test of strength. I saw every side of that man; he looked like he had horns at times. He cried, lied, did drugs, robbed me, choked me. I was tired of the emptiness in my heart. I found myself alone, on the corner of the couch, often crying.

I was abused mentally, verbally, and physically. I'd done nothing wrong but accept him into my life. My husband said that I married him on the rebound. I wrote poetry, but my husband said my poetry was about Seals, and so he destroyed my poems. Everything I tried with him failed, but I was afraid I could not succeed without him.

That's when Seals, my angel on earth, became my angel in heaven. It started with an out-of-body experience. While lying on the couch and looking around as I came out of a deep sleep, I saw myself standing over my body. I was frightened. Wouldn't you be? My body was there on the couch and my soul was standing over me. Frightened as a mouse, I prayed. I had to pray my husband away. The Lord was more powerful than him and his devilish ways. I sat on the arm of the couch, crying about the death of my friend Seals. Then the walls turned to white from a powder-blue shade. The room got cold, and my tears cooled on my face. As I looked up, I saw my angel, with wings, wearing a white gown. The wings swept across my face, wiping my tears away. A feeling came over my body as I saw this vision in front of me.

I believe I was blessed that day, because I got the strength to leave that man. I've been divorced for two years now, and I've never been happier. But we have now become friends, in a way. I had to forgive him; I had to understand myself and how I had let him do what he did to me. Now I know I am blessed in the Lord. I feel His presence around me, and I'm not afraid to sleep at night. All thanks to my friend Seals.

Eydith Johnson is the mother of two, with five grandchildren. She is a self-published writer and resides in South Bend, Indiana.

Angel on the Bridge

by Karen Gerrity

*I*t had been a dream of mine to own an acre of land with a cabin and a well in the Rocky Mountains. After leaving Alaska in 1986, I scouted an area called Little Thompson Canyon in Larimer County, Colorado, in search of such a place.

By early 1987, I found a neglected cabin that had been foreclosed years before. It had been owned by an alcoholic Vietnam vet who did not maintain the land or the building. In fact, animals had gotten into the cabin over time and there was a huge mess to clean up. Despite the chaos, I didn't care. This cabin met my criteria and was in my price range, and beautiful Carter Lake was minutes from the property. I had to drive by the lake upon entering or leaving my subdivision, so I never minded the drive to work or running errands. The scenery was gorgeous.

I remember one such drive with particular clarity, a drive I made six years after moving into my mountain paradise. There was a bright blue morning sky dappled with clouds that greeted my two small children and me as we departed our quaint cabin in the foothills. It was January, and there was a refreshing chill in the air and bright snow on the ground. I secured my eight-month-old baby boy in his car seat and fastened the safety belt as usual. My three-year-old daughter climbed in the back of our Toyota station wagon and fastened her seat belt as well.

We were heading to Boulder, about a thirty-five minute drive from our home—a trip I had been making five days a week for the last four years. As we left our mountain valley and headed toward Boulder, I navigated the familiar roads with ease. A switchback curve presented no problems, so I felt certain that the rest of the drive would be uneventful. While descending down the road, however, the glare of the sun struck me full force as we began to head east. The defroster had not completely cleared my windshield, so visibility through the glass was hazy.

I decided to reach into the glove compartment to get a paper napkin to wipe the window clean. As I did this, I momentarily felt the car swerve a bit, so I steered to correct the problem. Unknowingly, I had hit a patch of black ice, a thin layer of ice on the roadway that drivers don't usually notice until it's too late. As I've heard it said, "You can't see it, but you'll know when you're on it."

The car began to swerve even more. I tried to pump the brakes, but the car was already sliding toward the side of the road. I quickly realized that we were going to go off the road and down the bank, and as the car continued to slide, it became apparent that the bushes that lined the road were actually the tops of trees. The car was going to tumble down quite a distance, and far below I could see a creek.

Usually when something like this happens, I reach over to protect the passenger with my right hand as I steer with my left. But not this time. As the car began to spin to the left and I realized that it would roll over, I laid my entire body across my son's car seat, which was just to the right of me. I don't know why I did it, I just felt compelled to do so.

It was then that I felt a hand of love envelope my children and me. It was undeniable. I felt certain that our guardian angels had come to our rescue. The car crashed onto its roof and then rolled over one more time so that it landed right side up in the shallow creek. The roof over my side of the car was completely crushed, and I would surely have been killed if I had not lain across my son. Incredibly, neither of us appeared to be hurt. Frantically, I inspected the rear seat, where I found my oldest child still strapped into her seat belt, dazed, but alert.

I crawled from the wreckage, unstrapped my children, and pulled them to safety. Realizing that we were all unscathed, I knelt on the ground to thank God for protecting us and keeping us safe. There was broken glass everywhere—and not a single scratch on any us.

I had lived in the area for years and never knew that the part of the road I was on was actually a bridge and that a small creek ran underneath. In cold regions, bridges are very susceptible to the formation of black ice because they are separated from the warmth of the earth. Road signs are usually posted to indicate bridge crossings, with warnings that icy conditions may exist, but on this bridge, there were no signs posted.

When the sheriff arrived later, he told me that people usually don't walk away from accidents of this severity. He also said there had been several accidents at this very spot that winter and attributed them to the lack of bridge warning signs and guardrails.

This incident catapulted me onto a spiritual path that I still travel today. My faith has become a source of strength that I cherish and am blessed to share with others. Even though I moved away from the cabin in 1995, I still visit the area to take my children swimming. To my dismay, the bridge is still not marked and there is no railing. I can only hope that the angel who guarded my family that day is still keeping watch over us and all who cross that bridge.

Karen Gerrity and her husband and children live in Louisville, Colorado. Karen is the executive director of The Dairy Center for the Arts and is also a poet and inspirational speaker.

The Accidental Angel

by Jerri Handy

*Y*ears ago when I was a teenager, I would lie on my bed and wonder if God was real or not. I decided to "test" his existence, and so I loosely slipped a toy statue into the bed springs of the upper bunk. I prayed that if God were real, He would send me a sign, and the toy would fall. Then I would know He was real. In time, the toy probably would have fallen because it was not anchored very well. Not that I'll ever know, because my fear that it would *not* fall overcame me, and so I took it down and went off to find something else to do.

Older and wiser now, I realize that proof of God and his angels are evident in ordinary day-to-day life, if you look closely enough. What I do know about the presence of the divine in my life is that there have been times when I didn't know what to do. Times like when my son, Joshua, was born with a major birth defect, or when I was told my second child, Amber, had been in a serious car accident. Or when I suffered through a painful divorce.

At such times people would assure me of God's love and help on the difficult journey ahead, and I knew that God was there. In those moments, it was easy to believe. However, after the initial adrenaline wore off, I would spend many days and nights alone. I was overwhelmed by the huge responsibilities of caring for two children, one who has needed fourteen surgeries so far, and one who was perfect at birth but at age six was in a car accident that left her right arm permanently impaired. Sometimes it was hard to believe that my angels were by my side.

When Amber lost the use of her right arm for two years, we did physical therapy daily, and then she had surgery seven months after the accident. She was in a body cast from May to September, and then finally down to a splint for her wrist for about a year after the surgery. The physical therapy continued, and every session with the therapist was a painful one. Fortunately, Amber is a determined young lady who faced her injury with spunk. The total use of her arm will never return, but the doctors have given her a twenty-three percent permanent impairment rating.

Amber began to use her left arm, however, with some amazing results. I prayed often for God to touch her and heal her arm. Her arm did heal much better than the doctors thought possible, but she still has the impairment. She never regained the use of her hand for writing—her left-handed handwriting is nearly unreadable—but the drawings (cartoons and animated characters) she is able to produce are really good. It is amazing to me—she knows what the final image is supposed to look like, and then despite her handicap she makes it appear on paper.

Then one day Amber began to draw angels. It started when she drew an angel for a baby who was ill—an angel to watch over him. Then she drew another angel for a preemie who required an extended stay in the hospital, and then for someone at church whose mother was ill. After that, a man who owns a local candle shop heard what she was doing, and she drew an angel for him because his mother had just passed away.

Amber responds to pain in other's lives by drawing angels for them; God is speaking to and through her. With her non-dominant hand, she draws these wonderful pictures. Amber's angels have been as healing for me as they have been for her and for those for whom she draws. I watch these wonderful creations come to life on paper, spreading joy and comfort as they take shape under Amber's hand.

And I believe.

Jerri Handy lives with her family in Portland, Oregon. A mother of two, she serves as Minister of Family Life at THE VIEW Christian Church. Jerri is a marriage and family therapist. Currently, she is writing a curriculum for adults who are new to Christianity.

Note: To see one of Amber's drawings, please refer to the Acknowledgments.

Angel on the Move

by Marge Boyd

I grew up in Indiana, where hot summers are punctuated with wonderful thunder and lightening storms. It can cloud up and rain buckets in a matter of minutes, so for my mother, scanning the horizon every Monday morning was the first step before hanging the laundry out to dry in the backyard. Hers was a well-ordered life of household chores: Monday was laundry day, on Tuesday she did the ironing, Wednesday was for shopping, Thursday was spent in the kitchen baking, Friday meant house cleaning, Saturday involved yard work and car washing, and Sunday was reserved for church and Sunday dinners.

We didn't own a clothes dryer, and the washer was of the ringer type, so on Mondays, if the weather didn't cooperate, the entire basement would become a maze of wet sheets, towels, and apparel.

We lived on a block where families had lots of kids, and my parents were very popular in the neighborhood, so it was not unusual for children to stop by our house and spend time hanging out. One Monday morning, Brian, a five-year-old who lived a few houses down the street, came to visit while Mother was stringing out the clothesline in a zigzag pattern from the house to the garage and back again, strategically positioning the tall wooden poles that would keep the lines from sagging once the wet laundry was hung. Mother began to talk to Brian about how she was afraid that it would start to rain before all the clothes were dry, and she pointed to the threatening thunderheads that were beginning to roll in.

Once the line was ready, Mother left Brian and headed to the basement for the first load of laundry ready for its "fresh" cycle. As she climbed back up the stairs with her basket and wooden clothespins, she thought she heard Brian talking to someone, but she couldn't figure out who would be in the backyard with him. At the landing, she paused to listen.

"God, Mrs. Boyd has laundry to do today, and she needs to hang it outside to dry. So could you move those clouds over just a little bit? That's it, God . . . yeah . . . just a little more . . . okay, I think that's good."

When Mother, now grinning broadly, pushed open the back door and came outside, Brian said, "Okay, Mrs. Boyd, it'll be all right for you to hang out the clothes."

It wasn't until late afternoon, as Mother was taking the clothesline down and putting away the poles, that the first drops of rain began to fall.

When asked if I had any guardian angel stories to share, I wanted so much to be able to relate some inspiring—some significant event in my life. But the more I thought about it and the harder I tried to come up with something, the more I realized that there really wasn't anything that stands out— no near-death experiences, no narrow escapes, no phoenix out of the ashes.

Yet, in day to day events, I feel watched over, and there are many times when, if my eyes are open, I can see the clouds "moving over just a little bit." There have been times when I've worried about running out of gas while driving in rural areas where gas stations are few and far between, but I've never been stranded. It seems that every time I've needed change for a pay phone or parking meter, I've found extra quarters in the car seat or in the nether regions of my purse. When I've been uptight about running out of time getting ready for dinner guests, they've been blessedly late in arriving. After a bad day at work where one more problem would undo my composure and professionalism, someone else has needed my help, which ultimately put my "thorns" into perspective.

Then there are the times I've tried to lose weight and was led into temptation—by pastries in the lunchroom—and was delivered from evil, as someone else got there first and ate the last one. At times, when I've had enough of the Oregon rain, there has been a rainbow, and when I've had it up to here, someone makes me laugh or gives me a hug.

I think guardian angels perch on my bookshelf, on the rearview mirror of my car, on my computer, or by the refrigerator. I think they are subtle and watchful; they make adjustments but don't interfere with the master plan. I think they have a sense of humor and can be mischievous, yet are deeply compassionate. I think they are constant and ever present and manifest themselves in many different ways. I think they work through people, through nature, through our emotions and intellect. I think they place wonderful experiences in our paths, but also help draw us up by our own bootstraps for our own good.

Because it's probably not in the nature of guardian angels to knock us over the head and say, "*Helloo*," I'm sure we miss lots of guardian angel moments. In fact, I can picture my guardian angel sitting on my shoulder, with her elbows on her knees and her head in her hands, mumbling to herself about my stubborn nature and my inability to have the faith of Brian, who assured Mother that her clothes would be safe. He could see that bevy of guardian angels circling above my parents' backyard, flapping their wings for eight hours, keeping the rain clouds at bay.

On my good days, I can see them, too.

Marge Boyd, a mortgage loan underwriter, lives with her life partner in Portland, Oregon. She is a recently certified open-water diver and plays cello in her church's praise and worship band.

Angel of Light

by Lyn Wilkinson

My dad is the epitome of strength and caring. Many of my childhood memories revolve around him working in the summer garden, creating driveway ice rinks for my siblings and me in the winter, and teaching me to dance by having me stand on his feet.

A number of years ago, his health began to deteriorate. First, it was discovered that he had cancer in one of his kidneys, and then while waiting for his operation, he endured several unexplainable "attacks" that caused pain and restricted his movement. His doctors couldn't come up with a medical reason for these attacks, so it was decided he was having anxiety issues, which might have made sense—if it were anyone but my father.

Our family struggled to make sense of this odd diagnosis. Anxiety just didn't fit. My father is the calmest person I have ever known! Nonetheless, his surgery eventually proceeded, and he had the kidney removed. His recovery was remarkable, and he was released from the hospital within days. We cele-brated his amazing recuperative strength, and were delighted that his mysterious attacks would finally be over.

A few days after dad had arrived home, I received a fren-zied call at work from one of my neighbors. Dad was being taken back to the hospital in an ambulance, and my mother was out walking the dog and couldn't be found. I sped to the hospital, frantically dialing my mother's number on my cell phone over and over. When I burst into the emergency room, I was led immediately to my dad's side, where he was connected to several intimidating machines. Still, he seemed to be comfortable. The doctor informed me that dad had suffered an embolism from his kidney surgery and would be kept under observation for the night. The next day, it was discovered that dad would require bypass surgery.

He had not been having anxiety or panic attacks, as they had previously diagnosed—he had been having heart attacks!

As a result of the embolism, Dad was placed on a waiting list, and we nervously anticipated a call from the hospital to schedule his surgery. For more than five months, we watched him lose massive amounts of weight. He weakened very quickly. He could no longer sail his beloved boat or work in the yard.

He couldn't even manage a walk around the block. The wait for his operation became endless, and we were petrified that we were watching him die. He needed that surgery—and he needed it soon.

Summer approached, and so did my family's annual trip to visit my husband's family cottage in Ontario, Canada. I did not want to go. I was scared that Dad would die while I was away, or that his surgery date would finally be scheduled and I wouldn't be there to support Mum. My husband insisted I go on the trip, saying I needed to spend that time with our children and take a break from the daily pressure that life-threatening trauma provides. My parents both encouraged me to go as well, reminding me that I was only a phone call away.

After extracting a promise from my husband that I could return home immediately if anything happened, I reluctantly agreed to go. Of course, within days of my arrival in Ontario, my mum called to tell me that Dad was going to have his operation the next day. I couldn't make it home in time, but she promised she would call immediately after the surgery was over. I didn't sleep all night.

The next morning, I walked a mile or so to a little church on the other side of the lake. It was a hot day and I remember how long the journey seemed to take, each step slow, mired by thoughts of worry and angst. When I finally arrived at the church, I went inside. It was cool and dim as I slipped into a pew and knelt to pray. I'm not sure how long I was there, but I slowly became aware of a feeling of calm—as if I were being hugged. It was an overwhelming feeling of strength and compassion.

As I looked up, I saw before me a barrage of glorious color cutting through the dark interior of the hollow room. A prism of red, blue, green, and yellow from a stained-glass window high above the walls mingled and melted into the apse.

The rainbow of color bore through me, tightening its wondrous embrace. Whatever had a hold of me had felt my need, and I knew then that it was time to return to the cottage.

I left the church and walked back to the cottage, this time not noticing the heat or the length of my journey. As I arrived, the phone was ringing. It was Mum. My dad was safely out of surgery and he already looked better. The doctors would be keeping him in a drug-induced coma for a few days, and he wouldn't be roused until the day I was scheduled to return. The feeling of relief was intense, and I finally broke down and cried.

Today, I can look at my dad and see instantly that the strong man I'd known all my life is back. He recently took up playing the trumpet with a Navy veteran's band, and he marches proudly in parades wearing a silly sailor suit. He sails, he gardens, and he lives life to the fullest.

Although the trauma has passed, I still remember that feeling in the little church with utmost clarity. I had not been in that church in all the years we'd been vacationing at the cottage, but on that particular morning, I was called there. My guardian angel was there to offer me the comfort and strength I needed at a time when I needed it most.

A simple ray of light through a pantheon of color provided solace during a dark time, and for that I will always be grateful.

Lyn Wilkinson lives with her two children in the picturesque village of Steveston in British Columbia. She is an elementary school music teacher and a jazz enthusiast.

White-Water Angel

by Dale Erwin

*O*ver the past two decades, guided white-water rafting trips on the South Fork of California's American River have become a hair-raising and wildly popular adventure, so much so that restrictions have been put into place to control congestion and ensure safety. Thirty-five years earlier, I had my own hair-raising experience on this exciting twenty-one-mile stretch of rapids, an experience that transcended human restrictions and interventions.

A group of friends and I had just passed our teen years in the mid-1960s. We were an adventurous bunch, and after dozens of summertime trips down the South Fork, we considered ourselves to be seasoned white-water rafters—had we bothered to consider such a thing. In fact, we regarded our forays on the river to be little more than fishing expeditions with a few thrills on the side. Native rainbow trout lurked in the quieter runs and pools in the nether regions of the river, and plowing through a few dozen class III and IV rapids was the only practical way to get to them. Of course, in those days we wouldn't have known the difference between a class IV white-water rapid (which is a technical river designation meaning "pretty darned scary") and a class IV mechanical tolerance chart. I now believe that our cavalier attitude about rafting the river had more to do with divine protection than it did with any real skill on our part.

We all lived in Placerville, a historical gold mining town in the foothills just west of Sacramento, and a half-hour drive from our river getaway. Although others rarely rafted the river, it had become a familiar playground for us. The idea of paying for a guided rafting trip would have been as bizarre to us as hiring our girlfriends' fathers to chaperone Friday night dates.

The winter of 1967 brought massive snowstorms to the Sierra Nevada Mountains in northern California, and after a savage four-day outburst in late March, the high mountains were buried under eight feet of snow. My friend Chris and I were delighted. Our skiing excursions that year would continue into May, with occasional rain showers turning the normally dense snowpack known as "Sierra cement" into an icy super-slide. Most skiers prefer to ski in light, fluffy powder. We loved skiing on icy slopes for one simple reason: You go a lot faster.

As the weather warmed in the last few days of May, the normal thunderstorms for that time of year were heavy and frequent. Rain on the warming Sierra slopes was triggering the annual snowmelt, and the combination created runoff of grand proportions. Rivulets became surging streams, creeks became narrow swift rivers, and the series of dam-controlled reservoirs in the high mountains were filling quickly.

Our usual rafting departure point was just below the Chili Bar Powerhouse close to town, and the last control dam and reservoir on the South Fork before it makes its way downstream to Folsom Lake, twenty-one miles away.

One afternoon in the first week of June, Chris and I took a quick trip to Chili Bar to check out the water flow. It was flowing all right. Thundering cascade might be a more accurate description. Once again, we were delighted, and swore we'd be the year's first river expedition on an overnight fishing junket. On the way back to Placerville, I suggested that we stop by my place to take my battered army surplus raft out of the garage for a tune-up. Chris smiled and said, "Let's go to my folks' place instead. I've got something to show you."

We drove to his parents' home, where Chris led me into the garage. On the floor sat a brand-new, fully inflated Avon raft. Avon was, and still is, notorious for building expensive, bulletproof rafts, and although I'd never seen one before, I knew the reputation. This one had a wooden transom built for a thirty-five-horsepower outboard, wooden seats, reinforced oarlocks, and an outer skin as tough as rhino hide. I was impressed.

"I've been saving up for it," Chris laughed. "Get your gear together, and we'll go first thing in the morning." We were as giddy as puppies.

The next morning, we hucked sleeping bags, spinning rods, and small packs of personal gear into the back of my pickup, strapped on the raft, and hit the road.

Because these trips required a two-vehicle tag team, Chris followed me in his own truck. We would drive to our take-out destination near Folsom Lake, park his pickup close to the river, and then we'd take my truck up to Chili Bar to unload.

The South Fork normally slowed to a snail's pace as it widened and flowed into Folsom Lake. As we secured his truck alongside the road, we noticed that the river was flowing at a snail with a broken leg's pace. A bit nonplused, we made our way back up to Chili Bar. As we pulled into the gravel staging area just below the dam, we stared at the river and exchanged horrified looks.

Overnight, our thundering cascade had become a placid river flowing at a matronly speed.

"My garden hose runs faster than this," I said disgustedly.

"Must be holding back the water for some reason," said Chris. "Maybe the reservoirs aren't full yet." We stared some more.

Resigned, I finally said, "Well, we're here, and we're better prepared than the Titanic. Let's go catch some fish." I knew Chris was disappointed. The maiden voyage of his new raft was going to be about as exhilarating as a bubble bath.

We floated along for hour after monotonous hour, drift fishing and lazing on the gunwales of the raft. "Remember Tom Sawyer on the Mississippi?" I asked. "Well, Tom Sawyer was an idiot. This is boring."

Chris nodded, threaded a night crawler onto a fishhook, and casually tossed it over the side. "Yup."

At this mundane pace, we knew we wouldn't make it to our usual camping site before dark, so we paddled to the bank, pulled the raft ashore, and set up camp.

Pretty much by accident, we'd caught a few trout for dinner, and we speared them with green twigs to roast like marshmallows over the flames. We boiled a cup of water, set a handful of rice to simmering, and in twenty minutes we were eating seasoned rice and charred trout with our fingers— happy savages in the wilderness. We'd missed our wild ride, but we still loved this river and were at peace with our surroundings and ourselves. Just after dark, we stoked the fire one last time and turned in.

Hours later, we were both jolted awake by a gust of wind. "What was that?" I asked. I could see Chris shaking his head in the starlight.

"Dunno." The wind had died away, and it was dead calm again. A little edgy, we both crawled out of our bags, and Chris poked the dying embers of the campfire with a stick. We both sat down, looking at the coals, dozing. After a few minutes, Chris said, "I'm crawling back in my bag. Don't start whistling again."

Suddenly, we were enveloped by a flash of light. Not the popping of an ember light, or a flashlight, or *even* a flood-light. For a few seconds, it was as bright as daylight. I could see Chris staring wide-eyed back at me with the same look of astonishment that I'm sure I had. I could see the river behind him just as clearly as I'd ever seen anything. Then it was gone. I shook my head and rubbed my eyes until my night vision returned. We sat as still and speechless as church mice.

"Maybe it was a helicopter searchlight," I ventured.

Chris said, "I didn't hear any helicopter." Neither had I.

"Airplane?" I couldn't see him, but I could feel him looking at me like I was an idiot. Same answer.

The gentle sound of the river flowing a few yards away seemed to go up a decibel. We had become attuned to changes in wilderness sounds over the years. We both cocked our heads and listened. The sound of the river became a little louder. Then a little louder still.

Literally on cue, and without a spoken word, we leapt to our feet, picked up our gear and raced to the raft. We threw everything inside, grabbed the ropes attached to the gun-wales, and started running, dragging the raft away from the river as fast as we could. We pulled it up a small embankment, ran a few yards, and pulled it up another embankment. I thought the increasing sound of thunder in my ears was my own pounding heart, but as we finally collapsed, gasping for air and too exhausted to go further, the torrent came. In the dim light, we could see a wall of water racing along the surface of the placidly running river, completely submerging the banks from which we had just escaped.

After regaining some of our breath and a little of our composure, we tried to speak over the roar. We were too tired to shout and gave it up. Chris started giggling, then laughing to himself, and then was soon laughing hysterically. It was the maniacal laugh of the recently spared and seriously relieved. It was infectious, and I joined in. We laughed till we were wiping tears from our eyes.

"That was great!" shouted Chris.

"Yeah. I think we're going to be happy we've got this new bulletproof raft with us tomorrow!" We laughed some more.

In the morning, after a fitful night's sleep on the high banks, the river was still roaring like a pride of angry lions. We geared up for the remainder of our trip. We got our thrills that morning, and we blasted through what would normally have been a three-hour ride in less than two. To pull up close to Chris' pickup, we had to paddle like demons and hang for dear life onto branches along the shoreline. Still, we were swept past it by a quarter of a mile.

We had survived. Better yet, we had bragging rights and a great story to tell our friends and families. After recounting the tale for the umpteenth time, I grew tired of the skepticism that the "bright light" portion provoked. Chris had the same experience, and although we knew in our hearts how blessed we were by this warning, we began avoiding the issue. We discussed it several times, but we eventually let it go—a shared reality that we preferred to keep to ourselves.

We later discovered that the electric company that controlled the upstream dams had arranged to reduce the water flow for a day to do repairs on a hydroelectric system. After the repairs had been made (on the day we made our trip), the flow was increased back to nearly full capacity to reduce pressure on the rapidly filling reservoirs, explaining our midnight wall of water.

While we tried to pass off the gust of wind that awakened us as either a coincidence or air pressure changes caused by the advancing water, Chris and I knew that this was a first sign of the danger to come. Our bright light? There is no earthly explanation, but that was the signal that kept us alert and, I'm certain, alive. Early snowmelt water temperatures can cause hypothermia and drowning within minutes. Caught sleeping and trapped in our sleeping bags, we're certain beyond a doubt that we would have perished.

I'm a skeptic by nature. If aliens exist, I doubt that they would waste their time fooling around with earthlings (and if they do, they're probably "loser" aliens being punished for some intergalactic screwup). As far as Bigfoot is concerned, I'm sure that the evidence is a series of clever hoaxes, and I wish I'd thought of it first.

Yet on the South Fork of the American River in the summer of 1967, I don't doubt for a moment that my guardian angel, Chris' guardian angel, or an angel pulling double duty, flipped on a light switch in the night sky for a few moments, warning us to pay attention, trust our instincts, and take care of ourselves. I've been paying attention ever since.

Dale Erwin lives in Folsom, California. He has replaced whitewater rafting with the slightly more cautious pastimes of playing with motorcycles and horses.

The Courageous Angel

by Renee Evans

I know there was an angel looking over me that day. It was a slow day at work, and I had decided to take a long lunch so I could stop by a nearby health food store. As I drove up to the store, I saw two men running across the parking lot. One of them had a long, leather whip and he was chasing the other one, cracking the whip over the guy's head. I remember thinking: I really like working in Atlanta, but I'm glad I live in the suburbs and not down here with all these weirdos.

At that time I was twenty-seven, a newly-divorced single mom trying to learn how to cope with living alone for the first time in my life. There were many fears that plagued my mind, and most of them came from the teachings of the fundamentalist church I had grown up in and still attended. My religion taught us that the world was a dangerous place, people were not to be trusted, and the devil was constantly lurking, ready to bring danger to our door. The most fearful

teaching of all was that, despite those daunting circumstances, we could expect divine intervention and protection
in our daily life only during the hours when we were involved
in church work. God, we were told, did not provide individual
"miracles." We could only receive help from God for our spiritual efforts. Personal problems were our own to handle.

Having been a somewhat rebellious child and never really
loving my religion, I nevertheless believed most of the fore-
boding ideologies. I felt very vulnerable in life because, in my
mind, God surely would not be willing to provide an angel
for me. I wasn't completely sold on religion, but I had learned
that God sent angels to help us only when we were pursuing
some spiritual activity. It certainly seemed to me that I was
going to go through life without divine attention. By the time
I was an adult, my fear was so great and my faith so small that
I was afraid to really live life. I went through the motions,
hoping to avoid dire circumstances, and I always felt afraid of
what might be around the next corner in life. This, however,
was going to be the day that started me in a new direction.

As I pulled into a space in the lot and parked my car, the
two men ran farther away and eventually disappeared from
sight, so I dismissed them from my thoughts. I went into the
store, made my purchases, and then walked back out to my
car. The man with the whip was standing by the car on the
driver's side and the other man was standing by the door on
the passenger side.

Normally, I would have been seriously alarmed and probably would have turned around to run back into the store. But
I didn't run. In fact, I didn't feel afraid at all. There was every
reason to be fearful—there were no other people in the
parking lot at the time, there was no one to turn to for help,
and the two characters standing by my car definitely didn't
inspire me to peace. It could only have been my guardian

angel spreading her wings of protection over me, because I walked right up to my car feeling completely calm and unafraid. The guy with the whip gave me a menacing grin and said, "I love to get my hands on pretty-looking women."

At any other time, that statement would have been enough to chill my heart into a panic or freeze me into immobility. Instead, feeling the presence of my guardian angel and a newfound sense of courage, I smiled at him as you would some friendly stranger you simply pass on the sidewalk. I reached over to open the car door. The nasty grin disappeared, and a look of amazement came over his face. He stepped back and allowed me to open the car door and get in.

As I sat down and put the key in the ignition, I heard the other man try to open the door on the passenger side. Fortunately, I was in the habit of keeping that door locked. I started the car, put it in reverse and backed out of the parking place while the man with the whip stood there looking completely dumbfounded. I drove away.

When I got back to work I told my boss about the incident and he said, "You know, you really need to be careful. I don't know how you got away so easily, but you were truly lucky."

I thought about it for the rest of the day and slowly began to realize how narrowly I had escaped being harmed. Still, the feeling of peace stayed with me. My religious beliefs were deeply ingrained, but as time went on I began to understand that the calm I felt in the face of danger had to have come from divine intervention. I'm sure that the man with the whip would have reacted very differently if he had seen fear in my eyes. That's what people like him thrive on, and that's what he was looking for in a victim.

I'm now fifty-three and have long since given up my religion and its fearful teachings. I can look back over my life and see many, many instances of guidance and the synchronistic events that have taken me to the places, experiences, and people I am supposed to have in my life. Gaining courage, and the ability to live life and not allow fear to stop me from doing the things I want to do, has been an ongoing effort. I can't say fear never gets the best of me, because now and then it still does, but now I know, without a doubt, that angels are everywhere. You don't even have to believe—they are there, and they watch over us even when we don't think we deserve to receive their care.

Sometimes I hear an angel's voice whisper the answer to one of my soul-searching questions, and sometimes I hear angels speak to me through the voices of other people. But most important of all, I have come to trust that they will always speak to me, and will always help me find my way.

Renee Evans is a Georgia native recently relocated to Portland, Oregon. She is a practitioner of energetic healing arts and author of The Orion Chronicles.

Through the Eyes of a Child

by Pamela Hanke

*C*hristmas has always been my favorite time of year. It's a time for sharing love and laughter with close friends and family, a time when strangers smile warmly at you when your eyes connect. It's a time when all is right with the world.

I remember as a child that my favorite thing at Christmas—besides the toys—was the family Christmas tree. During the evening, I would darken the room and lay on my back next to our tree. I would lay there for hours, watching the kaleidoscope of twinkling color. It had a soothing effect on me and, often, I would fall soundly asleep. One evening, as I lay still and comfortable under the glittering branches, I noticed what appeared to be the shadow of a face on the ceiling directly above the Christmas tree. It would appear then disappear as the festive strands of red, green, and blue winked on and off. I was a bit startled, to say the least, and ran to fetch my grandmother. I pointed out to her where I'd seen the image, and she looked up and smiled. She bent down and gazed into my eyes and softly said, "That's just your mother watching over you from heaven."

My mother had died a month before my first birthday, and I had never gotten to know her. I was told that she loved me very much, and neglected to get help for a medical problem because she didn't want to leave me. Unfortunately, her neglect caused her death, and even though my father had remarried when I was two, I often wondered what she had been like and how my life would have been different if she'd been a part of it. That night, I thought about what my grandmother had told me, and I looked up at the face for a long while. I smiled and felt comforted knowing that my mother was watching over me.

As the years passed, I always looked for my mother's face, and every year it was there. When I lost my childhood innocence and ultimately entered adulthood, I still looked for her face, but I began to doubt that it had ever been there at all. I would think to myself, It's just a trick of the lights shining through the branches—nothing more, or, I guess I still have an active imagination. I would see her face, but my adult mind didn't want to believe it was there.

Many Christmas holidays from my early adulthood seem to be erased from my memory, and these are the ones where I doubted the existence of her image. There were no loving memories from this time period. No closeness. Only loneliness and emptiness.

Eventually, I married and started a family of my own, and with the birth of my first son, I began to see things through his eyes. He was astounded at the multitude of tasks that had become mundane and ordinary to me. I perceived a pile of laundry as work, but to him, it was a mountain just waiting to be conquered. A simple cardboard tube that once held wrapping paper became his sword, as he battled pirates on the high seas. Christmas, especially, became a time of wonder and sheer amazement as he discovered brightly wrapped presents, shiny ornaments, and twinkling lights. I became caught up in all my son's wide-eyed wonder and forgot about my mother's face.

When my second son was born, I was able to immerse myself in that childhood innocence once again, and one evening when my youngest was two, I found him and his brother lying on their backs next to the Christmas tree. I smiled as I stood there watching them, my heart overflowing with love, and that was when I remembered my mother's face. I lay down next to them, and as I looked up, I noticed her face appearing and disappearing with the blinking lights.

Again, my logical adult mind longed to explain away what I was seeing, but I wouldn't let it. I smiled and was immediately enveloped by that same comforting feeling I had when I was a child. I looked over at my boys and wondered whether they saw the same thing I had. I was going to ask them, but decided that it wouldn't matter—they looked content and happy just laying there watching the rhythmic dance of light, much like I had when I was their age.

Every year since then, my boys and I lie under the Christmas tree, in the dark, watching those glorious lights cascade above us. As they enjoy the enchanting glow, I take comfort in the fact that my mother is still watching me from above, and that she now has two more precious children to watch over.

Pamela Hanke lives in New Jersey with her two sons, Drew and Matthew. A self-proclaimed Christmas light aficionado, she still loves decorating for holidays. In her spare time, she enjoys surfing the Internet and doing crafts.

With or Without Wings

by Mardeene Burr Mitchell

*E*ver since I was a very earnest little girl in pigtails, I believed with all my heart in the Creator and angels and magical unseen things. In church, I prayed fervently for God to appear to me in a burning bush, but my responsible and grounded mother used to say, "Mardeene, you're imagining things." Of course, that made me want to see and believe all the more.

As an adult, while living in California, I sought out people, books, and courses that would teach me more about the unseen realms, but becoming involved with intuitives and psychics presented yet another dilemma. Why couldn't I see auras and angels and hear guides, too? I felt that as hard as I tried, I wasn't measuring up—that I must not yet be believing enough. I felt like a second-class citizen. My friends chuckled and said, "You're trying too hard. Relax. Everybody gets messages in their own way. God and angels are there for everyone. Just go inside yourself and listen to your heart."

I thought I was already doing that. Maybe too much. I was going through a difficult divorce, and I was becoming excruciatingly disappointed with two-legged creatures. As often as possible, I would run up into the California foothills to be with four-legged animals—my friends—and to be with nature. I would climb to the top of my favorite hill, my sacred place, and try to listen to God. One day, a young bobcat hopped out on the trail and ran along in front of me for a little ways before it disappeared back into the underbrush. I was thrilled. My writing friends—the self-proclaimed "Scribe Tribe"—dubbed me "woman who runs with bobcats." Although I found peace with God's creatures in this beautiful setting, I was still missing the spiritual connection I sought.

I was not the enlightened individual I longed to be. For example, when out on the highway among other drivers, I was a menace. Usually I am a good driver. Aggressive, because I like to go fast, but always careful. Even my elderly mother, who liked to be in control, would say to me in her later years when she could no longer handle the wheel, "You drive very well. I feel very comfortable in the car with you." Coming from her, that was saying something. But during this period of time, I swore every car on the road was out to get me! Have you ever had a bad car day? For me, it wasn't a day—it was a whole year of close calls. I even had a close call with a fire engine.

One day, my closest intuitive friend gave me a message from my spiritual guides: "It's taking a whole army of us to keep you alive!" I was grateful to be so loved and cared for, but I was still upset that I couldn't hear or see them myself.

Why was I the only one who couldn't see my angels? Had I not learned enough? Had I not accomplished enough to merit a visitation? I wanted to see my angels! Little did I know that was about to change in a most unexpected way.

One day, I was driving fast from Watsonville through the Santa Cruz Mountains, a highway with a huge accident rate and commonly known as Blood Alley. I knew I shouldn't be driving. I felt it. I was angry. Angry at myself, angry at life. I was even aware I was using the car as a weapon, a taunt. Screw you, world! I knew I should either slow down or turn back, but I didn't. As I sped along, I was doing my usual scoping for the California Highway Patrol (CHP). I saw no motorcycles, no patrol cars. Suddenly, out of nowhere, a black and white CHP car was behind me, siren screaming and lights flashing. My heart raced. Not good. I was already looking for a fight. I have a history with uniforms. I grew up in an army family. A loving family, yes, but too many damn orders to take. As I pulled onto an off-ramp to stop, I squared my shoulders, set my jaw, and prepared to do battle.

I couldn't see the cop yet, but I heard his boots on the gravel coming closer. I tensed. Then the strangest thing happened. I felt enveloped in a cloud of peace. It was as if somebody had spread a veil of calm over my Toyota Celica GT. I couldn't explain it. I just relaxed. All my anger had dissipated. I was a pussycat when the officer stuck his head into my passenger window and asked to see my driver's license. I willingly complied. He was beautiful. I hasten to point out that I felt amiable before I saw this handsome young man.

He spoke in a tone and manner quite contradictory to my previous encounters with the CHP. He smiled. "Now what do I have to do to get you to slow down?" It sounded as if he really cared about me. "Give you a warning? Or give you a ticket?"

He was asking me?

"Oh, please, officer, the warning will definitely do it," I responded. He handed me the warning, still smiling.

"Here you are then. Be careful. Have a good day." Then he was gone.

I sat for a minute, watching him drive off. It *looked* like a real patrol car. I was still calmly perched in the driver seat, in a ridiculously happy euphoria, wondering . . . Had I just seen my first angel? He didn't have wings . . . But I really knew the truth—in my heart. He was indeed the first of many guardian angels who continue to watch over me.

I have to say that the peaceful, protected feeling stayed with me for a very long time. I no longer had the urge to outrace every car on the road. Instead, I wanted everybody else to be safe, all thanks to a blond, blue-eyed, wingless guardian angel in a CHP uniform.

Mardeene Burr Mitchell is a writer/photographer, a collaborative author, and an inspirational speaker. "With and Without Wings" is an excerpt from her book in progress. Based in the Atlanta metro area, Mardeene has a mission to bring visionaries and visionary ideas to light to facilitate personal and global transformation.

Sadie Hawkins Day

by Carol Zapata-Whelan

I was squinting into the camcorder lens at a baseball game, taping Vincent, our eight-year-old son, trotting past second base when I first noticed the limp. As Vincent began to favor one leg, no one could have predicted that his strained gait was the first symptom of Fibrodysplasia Ossificans Progressiva (FOP). FOP is a rare genetic disorder that turns muscle into bone and, over time, leads to catastrophic immobility. It has, as yet, no cure or effective treatment. No one could have known that FOP would go on to prevent our son from combing his hair or tying his shoes. No one could have known on that mild San Joaquin Valley afternoon, as I pointed my camera at a spring-green schoolyard, that Vincent would have no more seasons of sports.

We have lived with FOP for six years now, always hoping for a cure and for scientific miracles from the University of Pennsylvania, the focal point of FOP research. But until a cure appears, we pray for an average teenage life for Vincent, who has traded sports for trigonometry and the trumpet. Although a sense of loss stays with him—with all of us—this loss throws the small miracles of life into sharp relief. One of these little miracles happened not long ago.

Last year, a lovely freshman with shy brown eyes, a girl named Clemencia, invited Vincent to his first Sadie Hawkins dance. One cold clear February night before the dance, Clemencia's family came by to take Vincent on a Sadie Hawkins shopping trip. Clemencia's parents, I discovered, were from Mexico, so we spent a good while rattling off in Spanish. By the time I got around to explaining FOP precautions, the teenagers had tuned us out, sparing Vincent the pain of my recitations. A few hours later, he and Clemencia returned from a trip to Old Navy, happily holding up matching khaki camouflage gear.

The Saturday morning of the Sadie Hawkins dance, the phone rang. It was Clemencia's mother. "My daughter wants to apologize," she said. Clemencia had the flu. Vincent quietly hung up the phone and retreated to the family room computer.

His older brother, Brian, was on his way to a friend's house to have cornrows woven into his hair for the dance, and his younger brother, Lucas, was at a basketball game. While I was glad for our other sons, my throat tightened for Vincent.

It was a sunny day, a clear blue one, in our normally white-skied valley, with the Sierra Nevada's dark rock and rivers of snow suddenly visible on the horizon. The afternoon was so pretty that my husband, Walt, decided to cheer up our son with an outing to a park across town that Vincent had never visited.

"Come on, Vincent," he said. "We're going to the park to feed some ducks!"

"No, thanks," said Vincent, expressionless at the computer.

"Come on," called my husband, moving our eight-year-old daughter, Celine, and our four-year-old daughter, Isabel, toward the garage with baggies of bread. He extended the invitation again. Vincent refused. Walt tried again. No answer.

Almost out the door, my husband asked once more.

"Okay," said Vincent abruptly. "But I'm staying in the car."

We found a spot for the minivan on the park perimeter and made our way to the oily olive lake patrolled by ducks and geese. Vincent stayed in the car. Our daughters had just started flinging bread chunks at the birds when a swarm of seagulls began to swoop and dive furiously for every crust, setting off a family laughing fit. "Vincent has to see this," said Walt, jogging back to the minivan.

From where I stood by the rocks at the lake's edge, I could see Walt rapping on the car window and Vincent's legs swinging out stiffly from the passenger side. At the same time, a pretty girl in sweats, with long dark hair, was running past. She stopped, and I could see by his posture that Vincent knew her. Walt discreetly left our son and his friend in conversation.

After a while, the girl jogged off and Vincent appeared at the lakeside. His face was transformed, radiant. "I'm going to Sadie Hawkins!" he announced.

The girl our son had just seen by chance was a friend from school. She had asked Vincent if he would be at the dance, and when he explained that his date was sick, she invited him to join her large group, which would meet at a grand new arcade restaurant—John's Incredible Pizza—for a pre-dance party.

Vincent wore his khaki camouflage pants to Sadie Hawkins, and that night, instead of a first awkward couple's pose, our son brought home a professional photo of himself in the center of a crowd of friends. As I mentioned before, Vincent had never before been to that park. In fact, it is on the opposite end of the city from his Catholic high school, far from our house. And the friend who jogged by? She lives in another town.

With the exception of that Sadie Hawkins Dance day, Vincent has never coincidentally run into any classmates—many of whom live in different or distant San Joaquin Valley towns. I said to my husband that afternoon at the park that I knew Vincent was surrounded by angels. Then Walt told me the name of the girl who jogged by at just the right moment.

Her name was Angelica.

Carol Zapata-Whelan teaches Hispanic literature at California State University, Fresno, and has been published in Under the Fifth Sun: Latino Literature from California *(Heyday Books),* Newsweek, The Los Angeles Times News Syndicate, The Rotarian, *and other international works. She writes to raise awareness about FOP, a rare genetic disorder characterized by congenital malformation of the great toe and tumor-like swellings that ossify muscle and connective tissues. Please see* http://www.ifopa.org *for more information on FOP.*

Jacob Wrestled an Angel

by Mary C. Legg

*I*t was Friday night, and the evening was clear. I frequently attend service at the Spanish synagogue in the center of Prague. It's a beautiful site, a mecca for tourists, and the oldest known site of Jewish religious observance in the city. But it sits in a city divided by religion and culture, where people from those different religions and cultures clash, often in violent ways.

I originally came to Prague after being offered a job in the opera. Unfortunately, the job fell through and I was hard-pressed to find the means to return home to the United States. Until that day comes, I try to make the best of a strenuous situation.

As a foreigner of limited means, I'm frequently caught in the middle of the tensions that threaten to tear this city apart. On this particular Friday night, I was minding my own business, just as I had been minding my own business on a previous Friday night when my landlord broke into my flat with his two friends and took everything they could haul away in the night, locking me outside in the street after Kabalat Shabbat.

The Catholics didn't help me, because I do what I believe and often go to synagogue and mix with the "unbelievers." The Jews didn't help me, because I am a foreigner and belong to the "enemy." It's this way in life here—people talk a lot about loving their neighbor and helping them in times of duress, but the reality is that the poor are left homeless and the rich step over them in the street. The level between the roof over my head and the street is pretty narrow.

But I try to do what is right, and therefore on this Friday night, despite the events of the week before, I set out to the local metro to go to Kabalat Shabbat. I was feeling very good. I had just received that all-important visa stamp renewal in my passport, and had only to arrange how to pay back travel loans to the lender in the United Kingdom, money I'd borrowed to come here, and then I could go home. Preparing the documents for the Foreign Police in the Czech Republic is a form of psychological torture. Although I was fingerprinted, and possessed a clean criminal record, the papers are more complicated each year. I am subjected to more outrageous demands on the amount of money that must be deposited into a bank account. The Czech government cleans up on all kinds of hidden fees in this business, and it usually has worked out a few additional fines to add to the annual kitty.

So I was happy, and preoccupied with my upcoming plans. Whether or not I was watching my steps, I can't swear, and the next events are blurred in my memory. I know that to enter a subway train here, you must be very careful to avoid tripping on the stairs leading down to the train entry. If you trip going in, you land on your face, with the doors closing on the lower half of your body, leaving you trapped halfway outside between the platform and the train. Nevertheless, I stepped into the train, only to begin screaming in agony as I saw the doors closing on my leg still outside. Someone had pushed me forward onto the stairs.

A young man rushed to me. "You can trust me! You can trust me! I speak English."

I stared up at two other men who were standing over me on the platform. Why did they shove me into the gap? Why didn't anyone push the emergency alarm? I stared at the young man. Why was he speaking English to me? What were these men trying to do to me?

Fearfully, I resisted the young man's efforts to help, and we briefly wrestled. Thankfully, he prevailed and pulled me into the safety of the train. The doors slammed shut. Stunned, I lay on the floor, unable to move. What had happened? Confused, I remembered coming into the train. I had been standing clearly inside the safety zone. How did I fall into the gap?

The people sitting on the bench next to the door did nothing. The train was full of people. They had all watched, but none of them had intervened. Struggling over to the young man, I sat beside him, shaking. We sat there together in silence.

"Should we call the police?" he asked.

"What good will it do?" I said. "I can't describe the men who pushed me. I don't know what happened. Did you see it?"

"I saw those men push you," he replied. "You have a bad concussion. You need a doctor."

"My flat was robbed by my landlord a few weeks ago," I said. "I have no money left to pay for a doctor."

"The American embassy?" he asked helpfully.

"I don't believe that the embassy would be able to do anything to help," I said.

We were both silent. My leg throbbed; I had been trapped nearly to my hip. There was a nasty bruise spreading like blood pudding where my leg had been twisted between the platform and the train. There were no witnesses. There had been no one on the platform to see what had happened. There were no security guards and no cameras. I exited the train when it arrived at its destination, and the young man helped me up the stairs.

"Where are you going?" he asked.

"To the Spanish synagogue for evening service," I replied, struggling to drag myself along. "I can walk...what's your name?" I asked.

"Jacob," he replied.

I laughed. "Jacob wrestled with an angel," I said.

He helped me onto the street. The horror of being turned into spaghetti sauce under a subway train was now behind me. Jacob had wrestled with an angel in the Bible, but here in Prague, Jacob turned out to be my guardian angel. With such angels on my side, I know that sooner or later I will make it home again.

Mary C. Legg studied dramatic soprano literature in Vienna and currently makes her home in Prague.

Are All Angels White?

by Sharon Johns

I have known from the beginning that I wasn't alone. Two events in my teens confirmed what I had known all along—that God's angels are here to help us here in our time on earth.

At the age of thirteen, something happened that should have really freaked me out, but it didn't. My mom and grandmother had decided to go to a different church one night, in hopes of seeing a "miracle." I had to get ready, so I went into my bedroom, knelt down before my dresser, and pulled out a drawer to find something to wear.

As I was looking, I felt a presence and turned. My room began to fill with what looked like gray smoke with no odor. Still on my knees, I remained turned, curious. A very tall man appeared, dressed in a dark hooded cape, his face almost covered, his hands clasped in front of him. He stood over me but never spoke. He stood there for a few minutes—what seemed like a very long time—just looking at me. He had a very peaceful and calm countenance about him. In the hooded garment, he reminded me of a monk.

I never thought about getting up and running. I just remained on the floor. I never felt afraid, just startled by his sudden appearance. He looked at me with kindness, stood there for a few minutes, then he vanished, the smoke cloud slowly leaving the room as if it had been siphoned out.

I quickly jumped up, ran into the living room, and told my mom and granny what had just happened. They went into my room. Nothing was evident, and it was not spoken about again. I was disappointed that they didn't see what I did and that they probably thought I was just weird, but I knew the truth.

Years later, when I was in my late thirties. I related this story to a friend. He told me of a Bible verse in Ezekiel that speaks of God visiting His chosen ones in a cloud of smoke. My angelic experiences seemed to happen in big ways, nothing subtle like the ringing of a bell or soft music in the background. The second angelic event happened when I was sixteen. My girlfriend, who had just gotten her driver's license a few months before, came over in her dad's car. It was a hot rod of sorts, and it didn't have a hood. We thought we were hot stuff.

We went out driving around town as teens do. We met up with a few boys, and we began to race. The guy in the other car took a curve too wide and hit the curb on the opposite side of the road. His car didn't just roll over—it went end over end, barely missing a guide wire and a telephone pole. As this was happening, we too began to slide, and I was casually thinking, *Oh, well, I guess we're next.*

As our car began to careen out of control, a most wonderful thing happened. In all her glory, a very tall, radiant angel appeared. She had very long flowing hair. What amazed me, in thinking about what was happening in the midst of this action—which is in slow motion for me now—was that I wasn't thinking about being saved. Instead, I was thinking, *Wow, she's a silvery greenish gray. I thought angels are supposed to be white, aren't they?*

She had the most beautiful large wings; they too were of the same shade of silver greenish gray, such a soft color. She had on a long silky gown with a long vest over it, as well as I can describe it, with a silky garment layered over the first gown.

She floated down with ease in front of our car. She took the fender over each front wheel in each hand and gently moved the car to the side of the road and stopped it. She had the most peaceful countenance, a calming, reassuring smile that radiated peace. She then disappeared.

I asked my friend, who was in shock, "Did you see her?"

She didn't respond, and I never spoke of the angel again. Who would believe me anyway, especially if I told them she was greenish gray? I have since found in the forest lichen moss that has a silver sheen close to her color and I found out later in life that silver angels are very high angels. She was beautiful and so peaceful. I will never forget her.

The boys in the other car must have had their own angel, even though their car was totally destroyed. When the police and spectators saw it, they thought for sure everyone in the car had been killed. Every one of those three boys walked away from that wreck, with no broken bones and just a few cuts and bruises. I've always believed there is a purpose to everything. There are no coincidences.

I married one of those boys. We have two wonderful sons and to date three very precious grandchildren, and I have seen guardian angels watching over them. They are there protecting all of us. It's normal, white or not, whether they appear as smoke or not.

Sharon Johns is a spiritual counselor, Reiki Master, and herbalist. "Are All Angels White?" is an excerpt from her book in progress. She lives in Braselton, Georgia, with her husband.

On the Wings of a Dove

by Tia Manca

$\mathcal{M}$y spiritual connection to my Grandma Maxwell really began on the day she died. This sounds sad, but I view it as a gift, one of the more beautiful, moving memories of my life. I was sleeping in late, as teenagers often do, and awoke feeling as if I were floating in water. I felt a complete sensation of peace and love, as if I were being lifted up and held, lovingly embraced. My grandma was floating above and around me; her warmth was washing over me. I was completely happy. Then my mother walked into my room looking shaken and told me she had bad news.

"It's Grandma, isn't it?"

My mother looked at me. "Yes, she died this morning." I was not surprised. I knew she had come to say good-bye.

And so my story begins with a gift from my grandma. Since that day I've had less fear of death, knowing that when you die, your spirit absolutely lives on. I don't remember whether my grandma was a "spiritual" person, but I think that she was smarter than any of us knew. We never talked about God or her religious beliefs, but I know she gave my parents their first Bible as a married couple. She believed in God and has always done her best to guide those she loves, even now, years after her death. She sends me signs to this day.

It started in college. I used to get the strange feeling that I wasn't alone. You know when the hair on your arms and the back of your neck stands up? The only problem was that I was always alone when this happened, and sometimes it would scare me a little—enough so that I would wish (okay, pray) that it would stop. I would pray, saying that I couldn't deal with it. Please stop! If there is information I need to know, please present it in a more acceptable manner. Give me a sign I can handle! That's when I began seeing the signs. Once again, I recognized them immediately as being from Grandma Maxwell.

I met my husband on April 18, my grandma's birthday. I gave birth to our first child, a daughter, Kaila Grace, on April 18, five years later.

Such signs thrill me. When I get one, I know that I'm headed in the right direction and making good choices. It also makes our daughter feel very special to share her birthday with someone we all loved so much.

Then there are the doves.

We have lived in five homes over the past ten years. All came with doves that made nests outside our window—even the three-story apartment building in San Francisco that had only a tiny window box on the top floor. Some people would not acknowledge this as a sign, but I remember that my grandma had doves as pets that she kept on her patio, and how much she enjoyed them.

Every time we move, I wonder when the doves will come. They walk around the yard and look into our windows as if they are just checking in, just letting us know that they are there. My husband teases me about my dove theory—he thinks that everyone in California has doves that make nests outside their windows. I've asked all the neighbors, and to my surprise and delight, they have not had the same experience.

So why is my wonderful grandma taking the time to show me signs? It's not that I think that she has been reincarnated as a dove. Here is the truth I've come to embrace: I believe that her spirit is now one with God and will live forever. Maybe she knows that when I'm feeling lost, or even grateful and happy, a sign will give me inspiration, reminding me that no matter where I am on my life's journey, God's love is always there for me.

Every time I see a dove looking into my window, I thank you, Grandma, for reminding me about what is really important. Thank you for comforting me in life.

My grandma was always a great comfort to those around her. How lucky I am to feel loved and comforted by her still. After all, the dove is the symbol of the Holy Spirit, of peace, renewed spirit, and infusion of energy from above. Could I have asked for a more beautiful sign? By showing me these signs, she teaches me that eternal life exists. Choosing the dove, a symbol of Christian faith, makes me a believer, a believer who is now raising three believers. I think that would have made my grandma happy.

What does a guardian angel do? In my case, she shows me the way, gives me comfort by making me feel safe and loved, helps me have faith, and makes me believe in God and eternal life. She reminds me to have a full heart and a loving soul, even when someone throws up on the new carpet, puts a crayon in the dryer, or leaves the car door open all night to drain the battery—all small stuff in the grand scheme of things.

Last week I was looking through my daughter's drawing books. One page instructed her to create a family crest, a symbol that would best suit her family. She had drawn a dove. My grandma's spirit is truly a gift that will forever continue to give.

Tia Manca is a wife and mother of three who lives in Redwood City, California. This story was written for her father as a tribute to his mother. It is her first writing endeavor.

How the Light Gets In

by Barb Karg

I never believed in angels. Not in the traditional sense. For me, angels were mythical creatures that wore halos, played harps, and floated gracefully amid silver clouds, marking the line between heaven and the hellish fires that burned far below. In my interpretation of this mythical literary and artistic phenomena, I supposed angels were guardians of the pearly gates who would welcome all who earned the right to enter. I'd considered them to be enlightened creatures, beings that could neither be seen nor heard, but who nonetheless held an honored position in the histories and legends of myriad cultures and religions.

To be honest, the concept—much less the presence—of angels was not something I pondered on a daily basis. My logical and scientific mind clearly overpowered my creative and intuitive notions, keeping me from further exploring the existence of such creatures. Quite frankly, the thought of a being constantly keeping watch over my every move would seem more disconcerting than comforting, and having seen *It's a Wonderful Life* hundreds of times did nothing to further my belief that I had a personal guardian.

Enlightenment, for me, had never been a question of divine intervention. *But what if it were true?*, I'd ask myself in a weak moment. What if there were something more to this mystical gray area of enlightenment? How would I know? Where would I be? Would it change my existence?

As irony, or destiny, would have it, my questions were soon to be answered, and quite without my knowing or expecting the outcome. People often search for ways to become enlightened, but in my case, enlightenment found me.

Many years ago, I had the great fortune of becoming friends with a chap by the name of Vic, one of those rare individuals endowed with a philosopher's mind, an innate gift of sensibility and science, and a strength of heart that emperors can only dream of attaining. His humor was fluid and poignant, and when he said something, you would listen, for his words resonated like the calm of the moon rising over a woodland meadow.

One rainy night in the waning hours of an ordinary day, we sat in my car, in the parking lot of a restaurant where we'd had one of our typical weekly meals. Our conversation, as it always did, covered the gamut from the wonders of the universe and the philosophy of mankind to the latest technologies and the true meaning behind the film *Groundhog Day*.

In all the years we'd been friends and colleagues, Vic was well aware of my intensely private nature and the elusive maneuvers that ensued when he or anyone else attempted to pry personal information out of me. This rainy night was no exception to that scenario. It was, however, a pivotal night that would affect all nights and days that followed. It was during one point in our conversation that Vic turned to me and said the single most enlightening phrase that I would ever consume. He said, "There's a crack in everything . . . that's how the light gets in."

A simple phrase, with a simple message, and while it may not have the same impact on other individuals, it was and shall always be the way in which I analyze the virtues and follies of humanity and, above all, the way I live my life.

Several years later, I received a phone call—the "call" that no one hopes ever to receive. My dear friend was not long for this world, plagued with an illness that was so quick and fatal that within four months he was to take his final breath.

Just after his diagnosis, I spent several weeks taking care of him, and it was at that time, during one of our lively musings about the reality of reincarnation, that I reminded him of his simple statement and told him how much it meant to me. It was at that moment that we both realized the ultimate truth of his profound implication—that under fatal circumstances, no matter where we both were, we would always have each other to light the way home.

To this day, his words and his light are with me always, and no matter the situation or circumstance, I know that his smiling presence is keeping watch.

Are guardian angels real? It's hard to say, not having actually seen one with my own two eyes, but I never did expect they were of true flesh and blood. Is this gray area of mystical and mythical proportion just a little less gray because of my experience? I'd have to say yes. It's a very personal revelation that has put my logical mind to the test, nudging me to question that which formerly was unquestionable—and that is not a bad thing. Did this revelation changed my existence? In a certain way, it did. I never believed in angels or guardian angels, but I'd be remiss if I didn't admit to the possibility of their existence. This is especially true for me during times when I feel uncertain or go into questioning mode. Perhaps it's just a simple coincidence, but more than once, when my mind has been unsettled, a form of light has presented itself—whether it's the sun breaking through the clouds on a foggy day, a candle lighting a darkened room, or a bright star in the midnight sky. When I'm feeling dark, light finds its way to my soul.

As the years continue, I look back and remember that this was not an epiphany that changed everything I've ever known. But it did bring out the best part of me, and I'm thankful for the experience and for the increased awareness of life, love, and friendship that might have lain dormant had I never heard Vic's words and lived through his untimely death.

At the end of each day, I'm still on the same road I've always been on, only now I'm much more aware of the destination. Whatever happens on my journey—through joy and pain, through failure and fortitude—I do know that a certain light will always point me in the right direction, and that light will bring me home.

Barb Karg is a writer, author, and graphic designer who is constantly fighting the battle between creativity and logic. She resides in the Pacific Northwest with her better half, Rick, and their five opinionated four-legged children. All six of them drive her nutty. On any given day, you'll find her sitting in front of her computer channeling Edgar Allen Poe or Mr. Spock.

Crossing the Bridge

by RD Larson

My grandma gave me a calendar picture when I was a small child. In it, a beautiful angel was shown shepherding a boy and girl across a bridge. It had been hanging in her house, and I loved it. At the beginning of a new year, she had given it to me, and my mama tacked it up by my bed. Every night when I said my prayers, I would look at the angel and the children and think about how much God must love us to send angels to guide us. I knew all about it because Mama told me that everyone had a guardian angel.

She said that my angel was very special because I was born with a hole in my heart. The doctors had told my mama and my pop that there wasn't much of a chance for me to have a normal life, and if I lived, it would be a miracle. My mother had to give me oxygen and prop me up with pillows, and I couldn't walk because of my weak heart.

I didn't know that I was missing playing and running around. I had my wonderful dogs and I learned to read because Mama taught me. I could travel everywhere and do everything when I read a story in a book. Sometimes I was really sick. Other times, I developed pneumonia and had to stay at the hospital.

When I was five and a half, Mama heard of a new surgery that repaired the hearts of little children even when it seemed unlikely and risky. She was brave, and believed that God had sent her a message, so she wrote to the doctor and he wrote back. She told me that she prayed that the operation would make me healthy and help me to live a long life. The doctors who first performed the surgery were all back East, but I lived in rural California. My pop wanted me to have the surgery, but we were very poor and couldn't travel back East, live in a hotel, and wait for my turn with the new surgery. So I continued to play with my dogs and little plastic horses with cowboys, and I still read *Little House on the Prairie* books by Laura Ingalls Wilder, but I was getting weaker. Some days I couldn't even sit up. My fingers would turn blue from lack of oxygen, and so did my face.

One day the doctor from back East wrote to my mother to tell her about a doctor at a hospital in San Francisco who was learning to do the surgery, and he had asked that my name be put on the waiting list. We were excited, but worried. Mama said she would pray and God would have it all come out right. We took the Greyhound bus to San Francisco. One of my cousins drove us in his car to my Auntie Edna's house. The next day in the morning we went to the hospital. Mama carried me, and Auntie Edna carried my oxygen tank. I don't remember much except that I had to be in a crib, not a cot like at home. I also had to have lots of tests that I don't remember now. That night when I laid in the hospital crib, Mama and I prayed that God would help the doctor help me get well. Mama then told me, "Baby, I have to go back to

Auntie Edna's, but I'll come back first thing in the morning and see you before your surgery. I'll be here when you wake up. You'll be all well, pink and healthy. You'll be able to run and play like the other little kids." Then she gave me a stuffed cat that looked like my barn cat at home. His name was Tom. She also gave me the calendar picture that my grandma had given me so long ago, and I sat crying and looking at the picture of the beautiful angel leading the children over the bridge. I could hear Mama's heels clicking away down the hospital hall.

I cried and cried. Finally, I looked at the picture of that angel and could feel her put her wings around me and help me to pray. She led me in my prayers and showed me the way to God's love that night when I was so small. I fell asleep. When I woke up from the surgery, the doctor said that my mother was waiting to come in to see me. She came to me and I saw her smiling with tears on her cheeks.

"Baby, you're fixed now. No more hole in your little heart."

"Now I can run and play like other kids?" I whispered to her.

"Yes, baby, and live a long life, too." Mama kissed my fore-head.

That was more than fifty years ago, and when I see that same picture of the angel and the children crossing the bridge, I still feel that magnificent love I felt for my guardian angel and for God the night before my heart surgery.

RD Larson lives with her husband on an island in the Pacific Northwest. She has had two books published, Evil Angel *and* Mama Stories, *which will soon be released as* Mama Tried to Raise a Lady. *Her work has also been published in* Guideposts *and more than 180 of her articles and stories are online and in print.*

Angels in Flight

by William Cassius Ruthardt Divney

Sometimes, as I drift off to sleep, I have this vision of soaring through a dark, soundproof sky. I am weightless and fearless as I glide . . . I fall . . . I tumble . . . I fly . . . .

I have always had a strong connection to birds, and have come to believe that birds are a symbol of divine love and guidance from an unknown entity beyond my realm of understanding. These birds, and the protection they provide, are my guardian angels, and looking back, I realize how significant their influence has been.

When I was a young child in a foster home, I escaped physical and mental abuse by pretending to be a bird. Lost in my own world, I'd flap my arms and run in circles for hours, happy to be alive. I felt free to be myself, and I felt totally secure. This was my only comfort, my only salvation for escaping the horror of my reality. I was also a chronic sleepwalker and had nightmares every night, so I assumed the form of a bird in my head, to let go, and to center myself.

I continued this "bird" trend after my adoption, at the age of five. Although my parents found it odd and charming, my teachers in grade school believed that I had behavioral problems because I flew through the schoolyard during recess, carefree and happy, instead of participating in sports. I was often teased for this. Once some schoolyard bullies pegged me against a fence while their buddies hurled ice balls at my head. Thanks to my sister, who folded her arms around me like wings, I was not hurt.

Birds remained my connection to the divine, and even as young bullies taunted me for it, two adults encouraged this connection. The first was my Nana Gertrude, whose encouragement was the driving force behind my father's decision to adopt us. He had some concerns and reservations about taking in "troubled" kids, but my mother was dead set on taking us.

Nana Gertrude was ultimately responsible for saving my sister and me from more years in the foster care system. Nana told my parents that God gives you only what you can handle, and she was right. She was our rock, and I think of her as a saint.

When she died, her last words were to my father, "Whatever you do, Larry, take care of those kids."

My adoptive great-uncle, John McGoey, was also supportive. He was an avid bird-watcher and, like my nana, was one of the most influential people in my life. We spent many hours together bird-watching, gazing upon the cardinals and blue jays who ate from the bird feeder that he built on his back porch. He was a great man, with a beautiful countenance, and now that he has passed on, I regret that I didn't spend more time with him during my teenage years.

Nana died when I was twelve, and my uncle followed her several years later. After they were gone, I often prayed to

Nana and Uncle John, and at times I'd feel my prayers had gone unanswered. Then, just as I'd start to doubt their presence in the afterlife, small miracles would occur in my life.

These miracles are always heralded by birds. Today, on many occasions, I see birds, primarily doves, staring at me outside. They take a position close by me and calmly hover. They are never afraid of my movement, and I talk to them, often with tears welled up in my eyes. As they meet my gaze, I feel a strong sense of serenity, and I know it's not all in my mind—it's my Nana and Uncle John's way of communicating in a natural way.

There are other circumstances where I have felt their angelic presence. On several occasions in my youth, I was nearly run over by cars, and each time I somehow managed to avoid death. I often wonder whether Nana and Uncle John had intervened.

The most notable experience was when I was twenty-three. I was standing on a curb, with my headphones on, waiting for the traffic light to turn green. Suddenly, I felt a push from behind, and I jumped back with surprise, wearing a typical New York attitude.

At that very moment, a huge SUV, going against the light, sped past me, punching my arms and sending electric flashes of pain throughout my body. Had I not taken a step backward, I would have been dead. The woman in the SUV pulled over and began crying, thinking she had run me over.

I was in shock and totally perplexed, but I know now that the "push" was an intervention that saved my life, as no sane human being would have pushed me into oncoming traffic. In fact, nobody was directly behind me, save for my angels— and a flock of birds.

I continue to have a great respect for birds, and am committed to fighting for their protection. It is one of my life's missions. As they look out for me, with my Nana and Uncle John's help, so will I continue to look out for them.

William Divney graduated from Performing Arts High School in New York and holds theater arts and public relations degrees from Boston University. Currently a graduate student at Columbia University, he is a director, actor, and animal activist. Based in New York City, he loves to travel, collect art, and do cartoon voice-overs.

The Language of Angels

by Evelyn Harry

I believe angels have visited me, and I can point out many times when such unexpected things happened that angels sent by God could be the only answer.

In 1989, my husband, Dick, our son, Keith, and I moved to Japan for three years of service with the Division of Overseas Ministries, which is part of the Christian Church (Disciples of Christ). Several times while we were living in Japan, we needed an angel to help us navigate the ins and outs of this fascinating but alien culture—and every time, an angel appeared.

The first day of our Japanese language class was the first day that Dick and I had ventured out of the house by ourselves. We had arrived in Japan on Tuesday, and missionary Doug Michael gave us a tour. On Wednesday, he taught us how to ride the train to our Japanese class building. Thursday, we were on our own, and we left our house at eight A.M. for our first class.

We walked to the train station, paid for our tickets, completed the train ride, and walked a mile to the class. After class, we walked back to the train depot. We had made good notes about where to turn, so we found the place rather easily. However, we had no food or water with us, and by the time we reached the train station, we were very hungry and becoming dehydrated. The temperature was hovering in the mid-nineties and the humidity was about the same.

So it was that we decided to search for a restaurant and have some lunch, but because we could not read any of the storefront signs, all of the restaurants eluded us. After a while, we finally found a restaurant with big windows and saw many patrons inside eating. It looked promising, so we went in, got seated, and were given a menu. There were a dozen or so items on the menu, which was, of course, printed in Japanese. We pointed to an item that appeared to cost about five dollars. We hoped that we'd ordered spaghetti, because we saw other customers eating spaghetti in a different section of the restaurant.

When our order came, it became apparent that we had instead ordered coffee. A single serving in a lovely English-style bone china cup, filled with coffee and a dollop of whipped cream on top. At that point, we realized that we had been seated in the coffee shop, and everything on the menu was coffee. We were disappointed and still hungry, but the coffee did quench our thirst, and it revived us enough to move on toward the train depot. Once there, we looked around at the many shops to see whether we could find a restaurant with real food, but unfortunately, we found nothing.

Our stomachs rumbling, we bought our tickets and boarded the train. Upon reaching our destination, we went to the turnstile to depart the station, but for some reason, the ticket taker stopped us and would not let us pass through. He instead pointed us toward another window. Confused, we didn't understand. We thought we had the same tickets that Doug had taught us to buy. We were hungry and frustrated, and I was almost in tears, when we heard someone say,

"Hi neighbors!" A sweeter sound I have never heard.

Our angel was a fellow missionary whom we had met at our apartment complex the day before. She was on her way to the airport to return to America on vacation. We had seen her only once, and we would not see her again for two years. She was at this spot at the minute we needed her, and we're certain that she must have been sent by God to help us.

From our angel we learned that the tickets we had purchased were about fifteen cents shy of the amount required to exit the station. The ticket taker had pointed us toward the window where, had we understood the problem, we could have easily paid the difference and been on our way. We also learned where to find food and drink, and that most train depots are located in department stores. If you go to the top floor of almost any department store in Japan, you will find a variety of restaurants. We thanked her, thanked God for sending her, and went to the top floor of the train depot, where we ordered a marvelous lunch and gallons of water.

After living in the Japanese city of Morioka for a couple of years we felt more comfortable with our life, although we really didn't have a mastery of the language. On one particular outing, Dick, Keith, and I were traveling to Sendai to update our visas so that we could continue to live and work in Japan. Sendai is a four-hour drive from Morioka, and at some point during the car ride, it dawned on me that at the place we were going, the Japanese Immigration Office, no one admits to speaking English.

For Dick and I, the process was a fairly simple formality. For our son, Keith, the process would be far more complicated. He had just turned twenty, which meant that he was no longer covered as a dependent on our work visa. Without a job in Japan, Keith would probably be issued a temporary visa, which would allow him to stay for only three months, after which he would have to return to the United States.

Keith really wanted to stay in Japan longer than three months at a time, so we would have to try to convince the immigration officer that he should be able to stay with us longer. A Japanese mentor and translator had always accompanied us when we went for visa extensions, but this time we had completely forgotten that important detail, and we were certain we would find ourselves virtually helpless with what was still a serious language barrier.

Filled with dread, I began praying that God would send an angel to us at the Immigration Office. When we walked through the door into the office, the first voice I heard was saying, "Evelyn-sensei." I looked for the voice and saw an acquaintance from Matsuzono Church whom we had not seen for more than six months. She and her husband were originally from Taiwan, but she spoke excellent Japanese and had a good command of English. They now lived about four hours south of Sendai, and she had come to this office today to obtain reentry permits for herself and her children because they were traveling to Taiwan to visit her family.

She had planned to be at the Immigration Office the day before this, but had not made it. Obviously, God knew our needs before we did. She was very happy to see us, but not nearly as happy as we were to see her. I explained our problem, and she stayed with us to translate for the entire time we were at the Immigration Office. Afterward, we invited her to go to lunch with us, and she graciously picked up the tab. I truly believe that on that day she was our angel.

When she left us, we thanked her, and once again, thanked God for sending her. We have never seen her again.

As visitors to a foreign country (where, in truth, we were the foreigners), the simplest tasks can quickly escalate into enormously difficult trials. In Japan, we were blessed with guardian angels who reduced our trials right back into simplicity. For that, we thank God, and we thank our angels.

Evelyn Harry is a fourth-generation Oregonian who has lived in Portland most of her life. Her hobbies include having adventures with her eleven grandchildren and three great-grandchildren, keeping the family's history and genealogy, and hosting international guests.

The Do-Drop-In Angel

by Heide Kaminski

They say angels come in a variety of forms and life spans. While some angels wander on this earth for a long time, many of them unaware of their celestial origin, others just pop in and out for a very short time. Just long enough to keep you from making a bad decision or to divert the sequence of events leading to a bad accident.

Two years ago, my family had a brush with one such do-drop-in angel. We had moved into a house just a block away from the town's police station and a few additional blocks away from the local hospital. The sound of sirens became a daily part of our lives. While they startled us at first, they soon became a background noise that blended into our consciousness, as did the regular traffic from a nearby major intersection.

It was a beautiful day in July. My infant son was sound asleep, and I was going about my daily household chores. My two daughters, ten-year-old Angela and Sarah, who was thirteen at the time, were on their way to the dentist to have their teeth cleaned. The dentist's office was right next to the hospital. As the baby was asleep and the day was gorgeous, my girls volunteered to walk over by themselves.

Soon after they had left, I heard the siren at the police station go off as I calmly went on with my chores. A few minutes later, the sounds of an ambulance indicated the nature of the emergency. Still, I did not pause to give it a second thought, until about two minutes later, when my phone rang. Suddenly I had a sickening feeling in my stomach.

"Yes?" I was almost afraid to say.

"Ma'am, do you have two daughters named Sarah and Angela?" a friendly voice inquired at the other end.

"Yes!" Now I began to cry.

"Ma'am, I'm calling from the beauty shop across from the Perky Pantry minimart. Your daughters have been in an accident."

I slammed the receiver down, snatched my sleeping son out of his crib, buckled him into the stroller, and then I ran. I raced the two blocks to the Perky Pantry. Other people drawn by the commotion reluctantly moved aside as I screamed at the top of my lungs "Get out of my way. My children were in that accident!"

As I approached the scene, my body was shaking with exhaustion, my lungs were about to collapse and the sight of my two little girls down on the ground strapped to gurneys with their heads tightly secured was beyond anything I can ever describe with words. I am sobbing as I write this, the memories are flooding back so intensely. I cannot imagine anything worse for a mother than to fear what I feared at that moment.

I literally shoved my stroller into the hands of a near-by stranger and said, "Please keep an eye on my baby." How often would a mother trust a complete stranger with her baby? I had lost all sense.

An Emergency Medical Technician stopped me. "Ma'am, you'll have to calm down before I let you talk to your daughters. They are fine. You are in worse condition than they are right now."

He handed me a paper bag because I was hyperventilating. My knees caved in as he held me up. It looked worse than it was. My girls were strapped into the gurneys for safety reasons. My younger daughter assured me that she was fine.

"Go to Sarah, Mom," Angela said. "She needs you more than I do."

Sarah was just whimpering, "Mommy, it hurts, Mommy, take me home."

The EMTs carefully loaded and secured the girls into the back of an ambulance. Because I had my son in the stroller with me, I was unable to ride in the ambulance with my girls, so one of the EMTs volunteered to walk to the hospital with me. From there I called friends until I found someone to come and take care of the baby. Angela had suffered no more than a broken toe and some abrasions. Angela's injuries apparently stemmed from her airborne sister knocking her over before hitting the ground. It was thought that this may have saved Sarah's life, and at least spared her from severe injuries. Hitting Angela seemed to have diverted Sarah from falling onto the pavement, and instead she fell onto the grassy shoulder of the road. She splintered a leg and had several severe abrasions, but her upper body was spared except for a deep gash in her upper right arm.

They had crossed the street feeling safe enough, and a van was blinking to turn left into the gas station as they crossed. Suddenly, a motorcycle appeared out of nowhere. The rider, upon seeing the girls, tried his best, but he failed to avoid them. He sustained quite a few injuries himself.

In the hospital, he and his family were in the room adjacent to Sarah's. His wife came over, crying, and asked if we were going to sue their family. We had no such intentions, as witnesses stated that he really tried to avoid the impact.

When Sarah was capable of talking about what happened, she had the most amazing story. "Mom, I did hit the road, and suddenly there was this woman. She picked me up and carried me over to the grass."

We were astonished. Who in her right mind would pick up and move an injured person? None of the witnesses recalled seeing a woman moving Sarah, but Sarah insisted that this woman had saved her life.

I sincerely believe my daughter, though, and I believe that for just an instant, one of those do-drop-in angels appeared.

Some people might think this angel was a figment of Sarah's imagination. But we know deep in our hearts that it was not. Sarah and Angela are here today, thanks to an angel who just dropped in to save them.

Heide Kaminski is the mother of four children and lives in Michigan. She is a regular writer for a local newspaper and a spiritual newsletter. She has had one book for children published, with a second one on the way. She is also a contributor to numerous anthologies.

The Unlikely Angel

by Izaddin Syah Yusof

*T*hat particular day in Primary One, the equivalent of first grade in my hometown of Kuala Lumpur, Malaysia, remains vivid in my memory. On that day, our teacher asked us what we wanted to be when we grew up. Most answered in the usual way: teachers, engineers, doctors, accountants, and police officers. When it was my turn, I stood up and said, "I want to be a writer."

My teacher seemed surprised, but she remained silent. Instead, she gave me a gentle smile and a wink and, without her realizing it, a truckload of inspiration. From that moment on, I won essay competitions, wrote for the school's newsletter, and even had an article published in the national newspaper when I was still in high school. Even so, I was discouraged from pursuing writing as a profession.

In developing countries such as mine, students are heavily influenced by their environment and educational system. We were tactfully tailored to grow up to pursue specific professions, i.e., "real jobs." Being a writer was not on the list. Writing was for dreamers, akin to becoming rock stars, or composers, or anything to do with the performing arts. So I opted to do what was "best" for me after high school by going to college and studying computer science. I now work in a large computing firm and lead a normal life consisting of regular working hours and fat paychecks.

Still, I did not give up my writing dreams altogether. After finishing college, I enrolled in a creative writing course, was published in an anthology, and had a few articles published online. Despite these minor achievements, I struggled to find the inspiration to keep writing. The satisfaction was simply not there, and I didn't feel that anyone actually had any genuine interest in what I was doing.

One day, my very close friend, Sarah, commented that I was taking my so-called "hobby" too seriously. I was both amused and horrified. Sarah and I had been very close friends since college, and even though we didn't have much in common, we developed a very close bond, one that is even tighter than my relationship with my siblings. Granted, we didn't agree on everything, but in general, we were always supportive of one another. That's what best friends do. I was surprised and a little hurt that she'd relegated my writing to a mere hobby, and more discouraged than ever. If my best friend thought my writing was silly, maybe I should give it up. We remained friends, talking for hours on end, discussing everything ranging from world politics to the types of cheese that go best on toast. We were always very close, so much so that everyone we knew from college thought we were an exclusive couple—they found our platonic relationship hard to believe and were always teasing us. That certainly didn't help when Sarah's boyfriend entered the picture.

Ray was never comfortable with the relationship that I had with Sarah. He never believed that a man and a woman could just be friends. I tried to befriend Ray early in their courtship, but unfortunately he had taken an obvious dislike to me. I don't blame him in one sense. Ray was clearly jealous, and more than a little suspicious of Sarah's being so close to another man.

As time passed, Sarah and I began seeing less and less of each other. Instead of weekly nights out, we began having monthly brunches. Sometimes Ray would join us, but I was sure he did so to monitor the situation. We'd be on our best behavior for Sarah's sake, but she and I had become acquaintances rather than friends. The friction between Ray and I was palpable, and it was obvious that the less I saw of Sarah, the happier Ray would be. Sadly, I realized that Ray's influence would continue to dilute one of my closest friendships.

One day, I met up with Sarah for one of our Sunday brunches, and we did some catching up since our last meeting. We talked about her new apartment, about the vacation that I'd just taken, the latest movies showing at the cinema—typical polite conversation. But then there was a long pause, as though she were contemplating whether or not she should say what was on her mind.

"You know what? Something really strange happened last week," she finally said. "You remember those articles that you had published online? Well, I showed them to Ray." She looked at me expectantly.

"And he actually read them?" I said, rolling my eyes.

"I'm serious!" Sarah blurted. "I swear I'm not making this up, but he said, 'This is pretty good stuff. You know I don't like him, honey, but your friend can really write. He should write more. He's got a unique style, and he's quite witty, too. Who would've thought?'" Sarah broke out laughing.

I was stunned and speechless. I didn't know if she was just pulling my leg. When she finally stopped giggling, she said, "I'm serious. I'm not making that up, and honest to God, he wasn't just making a mockery out of you." I was still speechless. Then she held my hand and solemnly said, "You are good, you know that."

This unexpected encouragement and validation, from the most unlikely person to give it, was balm to my writer's soul. From then on, I was inspired. Thanks to this unlikely angel, I had my "mojo" and could focus on my writing. Whatever success I now find as a writer, I will owe to this divine intervention. So pay attention, the angel who makes all the difference in your life may come in a form you'd never anticipate. Mine did.

The most unlikely people could be your guardian angel—just like mine was.

Izaddin Syah Yusof is a Kuala Lumpur–based bachelor in his late twenties. A database administrator by trade, Izaddin has just recently gathered enough courage to follow his dream and pursue a part-time career in the world of publishing. He also makes a great lasagna.

A Wife of Noble Character

by Rick Sutherland

*S*ix years ago I was an account manager for a bustling commercial printing company near San Francisco. On a typical Monday morning, I was busily juggling phone calls from clients, scribbling notes, and solving production dilemmas with my usual reserved ease, when an urgent call came in from my father.

"Rick, your mother had a stroke last night."

My world froze. The blinking red "hold" lights on my telephone console suddenly resembled the flashing emergency lights of a speeding ambulance.

Dad calmly assured me that the doctors had everything under control, and I really didn't need to break my neck getting to the hospital. A retired Air Force pilot, dad had flown rescue helicopters for years, and for many more years he'd flown modified B29 bombers into the worst hurricanes imaginable, gathering data for the Weather Reconnaissance Squadron. Calm was ingrained into dad's demeanor, and it didn't fool me for a second. I grabbed my cell phone and raced out the door.

At the hospital, I found that Mom had been moved to an operating room, where doctors were trying to relieve the increasing cranial pressure, and there was little to do but wait. Several hours later, the doctor who headed the operating team emerged and announced a partial victory—the pressure was stabilized. The bad news was that there was no way to determine the extent of damage that had already been done.

During the next few days, the answers to that question became apparent. There had been a lot of damage. Although she was conscious, Mom's right side was immobile from the neck down. Doctors were working with dad to help determine the amount of mental damage the stroke had caused. He brought familiar items from home: photographs, kitchen utensils, and favorite figurines. She recognized almost none of them. Her speech was slurred and largely unintelligible. One thing was very clear—she knew she'd been hurt, and she was deeply frustrated by her inability to move or speak.

Dad sat and held her hand for hours. I won't try to pretend that I understood the unspoken communications between my mother and father during this time. My parents had been married for forty-seven years, and now in their early seventies, adored one another as thoroughly as the very first day they'd met and fallen so deeply in love. When I sat with her, the only glimmers of recognition occurred when I took her hand and told her that everything would be okay and that I loved her. She squeezed my fingers and smiled with lopsided sadness.

Several days later, the doctors informed Dad that they'd done all they could, and it was time for us to take Mom back home for a recovery that they frankly felt would be very slow and never complete. Dad had contacted my big sister, living in Los Angeles with her husband, and my kid sister and her husband, who make their home in Oregon. They were all making plans to come to town to help with the transformation, when the unthinkable occurred. Being bedridden with limited mobility, Mom developed pneumonia. I had no experience with this cruel disease, and certainly no idea that it could so swiftly end a life. Within hours we came to realize that she would not be coming back home. And then she was gone.

My sisters and their wonderful husbands quickly made their way to Dad's place, where we hugged and cried and kept protective eyes on one another. I took time off from work and spent every waking moment of the next week with my family. My mother and father were never quite sold on the concept of cemeteries and gravesites. Instead, they had chosen to join the Neptune Society. This caring group handles the many details involved with the passing on of one of its members, and it arranged to have Mom's ashes scattered with lovely bouquets of flowers in The Bay near the Golden Gate Bridge of her beloved San Francisco.

During this time of grieving with my family, I found an unexpected source of support and genuine caring. Audrey, a young sales manager at the printing company I worked for, made countless trips to my parents' home, bringing meals, flowers, and best wishes from all. Although she had never met my mother, she spent many hours with us, listening to endless stories and fond memories of this truly remarkable woman. Early one evening, just before departing for her own family, Audrey suddenly asked if we had a Bible. I gave her mom's treasured old volume, and Audrey carefully opened it to Proverbs 31 and handed it back.

"This," she said, "is your Mother."

I read the passage with tears streaming down my face:

A wife of noble character who can find? She is worth far more than rubies. Her husband has full confidence in her and lacks nothing of value. She brings him good, not harm, all the days of her life. She selects wool and flax and works with eager hands. She is like the merchant ships, bringing her food from afar. She gets up while it is still dark; she provides food for her family and portions for her servant girls. She considers a field and buys it; out of her earnings she plants a vineyard. She sets about her work vigorously; her arms are strong for her tasks. She sees that her trading is profitable, and her lamp does not go out at night. In her hand she holds the distaff and grasps the spindle with her fingers. She opens her arms to the poor and extends her hands to the needy. When it snows, she has no fear for her household; for all of them are clothed in scarlet. She makes coverings for her bed; she is clothed in fine linen and purple. Her husband is respected at the city gate, where he takes his seat among the elders of the land. She makes linen garments and sells them, and supplies the merchants with sashes. She is clothed with strength and dignity; she can laugh at the days to come. She speaks with wisdom, and faithful instruction is on her tongue. She watches over the affairs of her household and does not eat the bread of idleness. Her children arise and call her blessed; her husband also, and he praises her: "Many women do noble things, but you surpass them all." Charm is deceptive, and beauty is fleeting; but a woman who fears the Lord is to be praised. Give her the reward she has earned, and let her works bring her praise at the city gate.

With tears falling on the pages of the book in my lap, I looked at Audrey.

"How did you know?" I asked.

She couldn't answer me—she didn't really know herself. It was, as she would put it to me long afterward, because a "presence" told her to turn to that passage. I am certain to this day that Audrey's "presence" was her own guardian angel, reaching out to comfort a family in mourning. I handed the Bible to my father, who read it slowly aloud to all of us in the room—Audrey, myself, and my sisters and their husbands.

It's difficult to describe adequately the emotional impact and sense of peace this passage brought to us. It will remain forever in my memory, and will forever bring comfort. I now live within a stone's throw of the Pacific Ocean on the Oregon coast, and I seldom look out over the crashing waves without feeling my mother's presence and strength and thinking about a shared angel looking over our shoulders.

Rick Sutherland is a writer who is currently at work on a novel. He recently cowrote The Graphic Designer's Color Handbook *with his better half, Barb, and is continuing work on several other collaborative books. He resides in the Pacific Northwest.*

The Faith of Angels

by Christine Grant

I have always been one of those people who has had an extraordinarily blessed and seemingly easy life. Things have always fallen perfectly into place for me. I entered this world into a very loving and nurturing family. I had a childhood filled with special memories, and I was a top student with lots of friends.

After finishing college, I found my dream job and married my college sweetheart. We both excelled in our careers and moved to a beautiful state where we bought our first home. Life was running like a well-oiled machine. After six years of wedded bliss, my husband and I decided it was time to start a family. It was an exhilarating and frightening time, given all the changes that were about to occur. We were both excited about adding a baby to our lives, and for me, it would complete the perfect picture I had in my mind.

Little did I know that this is where my "easy life" came to a grinding halt. Pregnancy, as it turned out, was not going to be easy.

When I first became pregnant, we were ecstatic, but that was short-lived. My first miscarriage was followed by a second several months later. By my third pregnancy, I was feeling guarded but hopeful, as my doctor kept telling us that the odds were still in our favor. As I passed the point of my first two miscarriages, I became increasingly secure in the process. My confidence was boosted by good blood test results and all the typical pregnancy symptoms. Nausea, food aversions, and exhaustion all became a part of my daily routine. The worse I felt, the happier I was.

In the ninth week of pregnancy, my husband and I waited anxiously for the first ultrasound appointment. As we sat in the doctor's waiting room on the big day, I observed happy and giddy parents-to-be emerging from the doctor's office with their ultrasound pictures. That will be us soon, I thought to myself. Visions of me pushing our baby in a stroller danced through my head. What will it look like? Will it have my curly hair? Will it be a boy or a girl? Finally, after what seemed like an eternity, my name was called. It was our turn! As the technician performed the test, she was being uncomfortably quiet, and I got a bad feeling right away. Then she spoke the most gut-wrenching words that I have ever heard:

"There is no heartbeat."

My head was spinning. I was in a state of shock.

"It's not possible that this is happening again," I muttered to myself.

We waited for the doctor to arrive. Unfortunately, he confirmed it. Our baby was dead. Life had suddenly thrown us another cruel twist of fate. I am a very religious person and have a strong faith in God, but this was truly testing my faith. How much more can one person handle? Denial, anger, and grief overwhelmed me.

After this third miscarriage, I was inconsolable. No matter what anybody said I could not be comforted. I was drowning in a pool of grief. The particularly hard part was not knowing anyone who had gone through what I was dealing with. Although family and friends sympathized with my situation and were very kind, there was no one I could talk to who truly understood how I felt.

One day, while I was talking on the phone with a friend, she said to me: "My prayer for you is that God will bring people into your life who will understand what you are going through and can comfort you."

Her prayers must have worked, because suddenly wonderful little angels in the form of people came out from everywhere to share their stories, support, and wisdom. People I didn't even know started phoning me because they had heard of my situation from a friend, or a friend of a friend. In one situation, my story had filtered through six different people.

The sixth person was a special woman from my church whom I did not know. She called me one day and told me that she had experienced a whole range of fertility issues, including miscarriages. She also put me in touch with another woman who had also experienced multiple miscarriages. In a world filled with so much turmoil and pain, I truly saw the compassionate and loving side of people. I took great solace in talking to virtual strangers about their similar stories and circumstances. Stories of other women and their years of infertility combined with multiple miscarriages were strangely comforting to me. I did not feel so alone. I also heard about their triumphs, as they finally became mothers after many years of frustration.

Hearing these women's stories filled me with hope and inspiration. As I talked with one of my "angels," I relayed how frightened I was to get pregnant again. She said something very powerful that I will never forget.

"Sometimes we have to view things from the eyes of a child," she said. "Children do not look at situations with fear and anxiety. They just trust and have faith that everything will be okay."

These words have given me a new perspective and helped calm my anxious heart. As I look to my future, I have a renewed sense of peace and a positive outlook. How magical it is to see life through the eyes of a child and to feel the comforting embrace of my guardian angels.

Christine Grant is a real estate appraiser in the Pacific Northwest, where she lives with her husband, Glen, and two cats, Bailey and Simba. She enjoys traveling and discovering new cultures.

Seeing Is Believing

by Tammy L. Nelson

I've always believed in the existence of another world, the one that we inhabit after we die. The belief comes not so much from the teachings of religion but from that deep place within yourself, where you just acknowledge things that you may not be able to see or touch yet know are there.

I read a great deal, and the subject of making contact with the beyond is something I've read about extensively. Several years ago, I read about guardian angels and how to identify your own, so I gave it a try. I mean, why not? What is there to lose? Several nights later, just prior to falling asleep, I had my first encounter with my guardian angel. His name was John, and he looked like my idea of a college English professor. He was wearing a casual suit and sporting white hair and a small, neat mustache. He had a dignified but utterly kind manner about him, and he was always sitting behind a desk in a study.

I pretty much went on with my life after that, not really thinking about it or trying to talk with John. Then about a year and a half ago, I became friends with a woman who reads tarot cards. She was quite insistent that I had some type of psychic ability, and she asked that I try to communicate with John. I guess all I needed to do was to open the door and allow him to speak with me, because it was like being hit with a massive tidal wave when I finally did.

I now often communicate with John during the night, and when I call for him, he is always there. On one particular night, John had much to say, and during our conversation, he gave me something. It looked like two metal tubes joined together, and it had a lid on it. When I opened it, a tiny pair of binoculars slid out. He said that they were for me and that I should "look closer."

I was skeptical of this entire encounter. A large part of me was sure that my mind was just creating stories. About a week later, I was visiting with my daughter at the kitchen table when my husband came home from work. I wasn't paying too much attention to what he was doing, but I suddenly saw something in his hands that looked oddly familiar. It was the tiny binoculars, case and all! I was stunned. It was one of those moments when everything felt unreal. It seemed as though John was confirming his existence to me, but being a skeptic by nature, I still had no idea what it all meant, and because my mind was focused on my father's health at the time, I put the entire incident on the back burner.

My father had been ill for quite some time and was under the care of hospice. This was the hardest thing I had ever had to face. There were days when I was sure that I couldn't bear it for another second. My dad was the smartest man I'd ever known. I consulted him about everything, and I knew that when he died I would lose my center, my pillar of strength, and the one person for whom I strived to be better.

He passed away at home on January 12, 2003, surrounded by his loving family. I held his hand as he left us, and my world turned upside down. I didn't know how I was going to go on without him in my life. Instead of facing the tragedy, I swallowed all the pain, locked it up, and refused to look at it. I was numb for weeks.

One night, my guardian angel John, came to me with words of comfort. He knew how badly I was hurting. I remember that I kept saying to him that I didn't think I could live the rest of my life without my dad there to turn to. What happened to him after he died? Was he okay? John simply smiled and placed his hand on my shoulder.

He indicated that I should look to my right. When I did, I saw my dad standing there, and he looked better than I'd seen him look in years. He had the biggest smile on his face that I'd ever seen. He told me that everything was okay and that he was happy.

I still can't think about my dad without crying, but I'm able now to "look closer" at our relationship and cherish all that he gave me, rather than mourn for what I will no longer be receiving. John is only one request away from me, and he remains, to this day, my true guardian angel.

Tammy Nelson lives in northern Wisconsin with her husband, Jeff, and daughter, Jessica. Tammy enjoys reading, painting, and her three cats.

The Kitchen Angel

by George Karg

As a young boy growing up in Germany, I always read the novels of Jack London. The thrill of exploring unknown lands and the adventurous lure of travel was something I could only dream of, especially during a particularly chaotic time in human history.

I was fifteen-years-old in 1943, and what should have been a normal teenage life, filled with dancing, courting, education, and sport, was consumed by the horrors of World War II. I'll never know for certain what pushed me into making the first big decision of my life, but it set the stage for a series of events for which I am most thankful.

Since both of my older brothers were already in the German navy, I decided that I wanted to be in the navy, too. I was ready to wear a uniform, or so I thought. I joined the navy in 1943 as a naval cadet and spent the next two years in a naval school in southern Germany.

In 1944, while still in school and with the war raging, I received notice for induction into the German army. By government demand, all the young men born in 1928—regardless of their current military status—had to register for the army and be officially inducted. Hesitant, I went to the draft office and was examined by army doctors. Despite being a naval cadet, I thought for sure they were going to draft me into the army because they desperately needed foot soldiers.

After enduring all the examinations, I felt certain my fate was sealed. All other kids my age had already been drafted. I waited anxiously, then much to my surprise, I was released from the draft without explanation. I was sixteen, strong, and in good health. Why wasn't I selected? Who or what saved me from the battlefields?

In May 1945, my fellow naval cadets and I were marched into captivity as a result of the French army taking over the area. The French detained me for more than five weeks, but luckily I was released after the end of the war. Had I been inducted the previous year, I would have never walked back into freedom. A guardian angel was looking out for me during my youth, whether I realized it or not, and that angel would continue to do so for a very long time to come.

My parents were both killed during the war. My father was missing in action, and my mom was in a bomb shelter that had taken a direct hit. I was sixteen, had no possessions, and had nothing to go home to, so I had to find a profession. The country was ravaged both physically and economically, times were very tough, and my survival instinct kicked in. I was hungry, and I needed a job that would provide food and lodging. The only way I could obtain that was by learning a trade, so I decided to become a chef.

After the war, I moved to Bavaria and started my apprenticeship as a cook, still wondering how I was lucky enough to have survived the war and be able to experience future adventures. After three and a half years of apprenticing, I started my journey. From 1945 to 1956 I worked at different restaurants, hotels, and resorts in the area. I always had food and I always had a roof over my head. In June 1956, I acquired a visa and took a two-week passage through the Mediterranean on a cruise ship that eventually brought me to Halifax, Canada.

My cooking skills again served my purpose, and I secured a job as a sous chef at an exclusive hotel in Kingston. The head chef at the hotel, who happened to be an Irishman, taught me English. As a result, I acquired his Irish accent! After a few months, however, the Jack London in me kicked in, and a friend and I took employment working in the tobacco fields in Ontario. Tobacco harvesting was a far cry from the frying pan, and so I decided to apply for a job working in a local uranium mine. Now at that time, in 1956, little was known about the dangers of uranium mining, and although I very much wanted the work, I was denied the job without an explanation. Again, my guardian angel was looking out for me because, with few safety regulations, working in those mines turned out to be extremely dangerous. Apparently, my kitchen angel didn't want me working in a mine, she wanted me in front of a stove!

Still fueled by dreams of adventure, however, I found a job with a company that was working the St. Lawrence Seaway. You should hear my daughters laugh as they think of their dad working on a dredge as a "grease monkey." Of course, that job didn't last long. When they found out that the grease monkey was a chef, they launched me on a tugboat, where I cooked for ten burly seamen. Again, it seemed, something or someone kept pulling me back to the kitchen.

When winter storms hit, all operations closed down, and I obtained a visa to the United States. I moved to Niagara Falls,

New York, and was hired by the Niagara Mohawk Power Corporation, a power plant that employed more than 10,000 people. It was the biggest construction site of its time, and I was just another day laborer running a concrete vibrator.

On any given day, I was working on various intake tunnels for the Falls, and on two occasions, they overblasted the area and a sea of rock rained down on the workers. Again, I felt the presence of my guardian angel, as I narrowly missed getting crushed to death. That was a hint I couldn't ignore. I was in the wrong profession, and someone or something kept telling me to move to California.

So in 1960, I drove from Niagara Falls to southern California, with its beautiful beaches and scenic mountains. When I arrived, I again had to search for employment, and the question was where to begin. On a warm June afternoon a few days after my arrival, I happened to meet an Austrian chef at a local bar. We started chatting over a beer, and he mentioned that he knew a club that was looking for a sous chef. Five days later, I once again was able to put food on my table, and the job lasted for eleven years.

I felt lucky being in this place, and grateful that I'd been led here. Being young, and in a new town, I was casually driving around one day when I happened upon a Swiss restaurant, where, as it turned out, all the Europeans hung out. The former German naval cadet who'd learned English from an Irishman had found a slice of home, and it was shortly thereafter that I met my wife of forty-two years.

From then on, I worked as a head chef in private clubs, and after forty-five years of cooking and adventure, I retired in 1990. Three years later, however, disaster struck when I discovered I had prostate cancer. It was at that moment, after so many years, that I wondered whether my guardian angel was still watching my back. As it turned out, he was. After several years, I had a complete recovery. In April 2001, however, I was diagnosed with colon cancer. Yet after a difficult surgery, I made a remarkable recovery and have remained free of cancer ever since.

I found out, long after the war had ended and the Wall came down, that the life expectancy of a young German soldier of sixteen was only thirty days.

I absolutely believe that I wouldn't be alive today if not for my guardian angel. I would have certainly been a casualty of war or tragedy. Instead, I have that kitchen angel to thank for keeping me healthy, happily married, and gifted with a close-knit family. I truly enjoy being a family man. My former profession is now my hobby, and I'm still cooking up a storm, and to my kitchen angel, I will always be thankful.

George Karg is a retired chef who loves to laugh, discover new kitchen implements, and go grocery-store hopping. He resides in southern California and often visits his two daughters and his seven four-legged grandchildren. Thanks to his guardian angel, he can still cook a mean goulash.

Angel Pop

by Josie Williams

I was a slight child. Only five pounds at birth and slow to grow, and by the age of seven I was only as tall as the average four-year-old. I weighed in at a whopping 28 pounds.

I hated being little and fought to be taken seriously as the solemn, mature second grader that I was. Kids at school teased me and called "shrimp." I was easily the smallest child in my class; even most of the kindergartners towered over me. Whenever the teachers lined us up for pictures, chorus, or field trips, they always said, "Let little Josie up front. We don't want her to get lost." It was embarrassing.

My mother was so worried about my lack of stature that she dragged me to the doctor for a "midget test," as she called it. To her great relief the doctor insisted that I was perfectly normal, albeit petite. I continued to worry that I'd never measure up. I didn't want to be treated like a baby all my life.

When I came down with appendicitis and needed emergency surgery, the doctors were worried. I was so tiny; how much anesthesia should they use? I didn't know what they were talking about, but it didn't sound good.

"We're going to give you something to put you to sleep," the nurse told me, patting my hand. "When you wake up, it'll be all over and your tummy won't hurt any more."

They rolled me into the surgery and a bright light shone in my eyes. Grown-ups with masks stared down at me. I was terrified. One masked man leaned over and talked to me.

"I'm going to put this mask over your face," he said. "Breathe in and out, and count backwards from one hundred."

"100, 99, 98, 97 . . . . " This was hard. I closed my eyes and tried to remember which number came before 97. I could not concentrate. Numbers swam in my mind; my thinking cap was slipping, slipping, slipping off, and I was out.

Out of my body. All of a sudden I was flying above the table, hovering over the grown-ups in masks who were huddled around a little girl who looked a lot like me. I looked closer. It was me!

I was scared. I didn't know what to do. I felt like flying away—far away from doctors and nurses and hospitals. Flying away to heaven, where everything would be nice and happy and my tummy wouldn't hurt any more, and no one would cover my face and make me count backwards.

"What about your Mommy and Daddy?"

Someone was talking to me, I could hear his voice in my head. He had an old voice, like my Grandpa. I looked down at the hospital people, but they were all busy, they were looking at the old me down there, not the new me up here.

"They love you very much and if you go away, they'll miss you. Go back, child, go back home to your Mommy and Daddy."

Somehow I knew he meant back into the old me down on the table.

"How do I go?" I whispered.

"Just count backwards," he said. "96, 95, 94 . . . ."

I counted along with him. "93, 92, 91 . . . ."

When I woke up hours later I was in a hospital room. My mother was there, holding my hand. I could tell that my mother had been crying.

"Thank God!" she said, and kissed my forehead. "The doctor says that you're going to be just fine."

I remembered what the voice had told me. "Where's Daddy?"

"He'll be right here, he just stepped out for a moment." Mommy stayed with me until Daddy came. He kissed me, too. I was where I was supposed to be after all.

As it turned out, the doctors had given me too much anesthesia and I'd gotten very sick. They'd nearly lost me, my mother said.

When I told my parents about the voice like Grandpa's, they said that I was delirious. I had to stay in the hospital for several more days. One night I awoke to find an old man beside my bed.

"You are a little thing," he said, looking at me.

"I hate being little," I said.

"Good things come in small packages." He smiled.

I recognized his voice. He was the man who'd sent me back to my parents. "Are you an angel?"

He chuckled. "Sort of. I'm your Angel Pop. Now go back to sleep."

I never saw him again, and eventually I began to believe it had all been just dreams, fueled first by too much anesthesia and later by a little girl's imagination.

But years later I found out that my paternal grandfather was also staying in the very same hospital at the very same time I was. He and my father were estranged. I'd never met him, and I never did meet him. He died not long afterwards.

My dad called him Pop.

Even though Josie Williams grew up protected by a large and caring family, an innate curiosity and a desire to climb everything in sight led to many injuries. After broken bones, countless stitches, and a few surgeries, she feels extremely blessed to be the healthy adult she is today. A passionate horticulturist, she continues to climb the mountains of New England, and thanks her guardian angels for keeping her safe.

Brandy

by David Michael Smith

The phone rang at precisely nine p.m., as a drought buster of a storm raged angrily outside our bedroom windows. Instinctively, my wife and I both knew who it was, and I answered the call with a dull numbness, as if I'd been maced with Novocain.

"Mr. Smith, this is John at the veterinary hospital," the voice flatly reported with a grave monotone. "I'm afraid things have taken a turn for the worst."

My heart sank and tears spilled from my wife's eyes. She could tell from my wooden expression that the news wasn't good.

"With your permission, I can do some emergency exploratory surgery, see if there's anything I can do to save your dog, Brandy. It's a long shot, but it's our only hope."

I paused, knowing there was more.

"But, the odds are against success, and if I can't do anything, I'll need to put her down," he added with a solemn whisper. "It's the humane thing to do. She's very sick, and she's suffering."

I felt like someone had sucker punched me in the gut. I couldn't breathe. "I need to discuss this with my wife, please, John," I managed, my voice shaky. "I'll call you right back."

I hung up and discussed the matter with my wife. We both agreed that we wanted to be there for our friend, for our child, to provide a comforting and familiar presence. For years we had tried to start a family with no success. Everything was tried during those tedious months, every imaginable process, method, old wives' tale, and suggestion, not to mention countless prayers of faith. But it was not meant to be. Some things just aren't. Each effort fell short, and our marriage, though strengthened by the experiences, would remain childless.

For the thirteen years of her life, Brandy was more than a pet to us—she was a precious jewel in our daily lives, a member of our family. She was a faithful companion, lovable, loyal, and humorous. We made the hard decision while wiping away tears, the humane decision, to bypass the painful surgery and go to the veterinary hospital in the evening rainstorm. We would hold our dear pet, Brandy, as she was given the needles that would help her pass over to the eternal side of existence.

I called back to inform the doctor of our decision. Strangely, it took John five rings to answer his cell phone, despite knowing I was calling right back. He told me he'd have the phone by his side. Finally, the call was accepted with an echoing click.

"Mr. Smith," the voice hesitated with great emotion, "your dog just collapsed into my arms. I think she's dying." He fumbled with his stethoscope on the other end while I listened to the surrealistic nightmare in my ear, wishing I would wake up.

"Oh God, I'm so sorry . . . she just took her last breath. She's gone."

The man was in tears. I soon joined him, sobbing like a newborn. Our drive over to the vet's office was a silent one until my wife suggested we relive special memories. There were many, and we found ourselves laughing, and then crying all over again. Our dog had impacted our lives more than we realized. Inside the vet's office, abandoned and quiet on a Sunday night, we thanked John for being there to hold our friend as she passed away. It was more than mere coincidence that he happened to be there that night. Moments later, our hearts were warmed when we saw her still, furry body. She was clearly at peace, as if she were merely sleeping.

After wrapping Brandy in cotton blankets, we laid her gently on the backseat of our car. Wet and still in shock, we slowly backed out and exited the parking lot with a reverent spirit. About a mile or two later, my wife broke the solitude with a loud, startled scream. I quickly asked her, "What's wrong?"

"Brandy just licked me! On the back of my neck! Honestly, I felt it!" My wife was ecstatic, thrilled beyond words.

I peered into the backseat, half expecting a modern-day Lazarus miracle, but, of course, Brandy was motionless and still wrapped in blankets.

"Maybe you just felt something, honey, a wisp of air or something," I offered, confused yet intrigued.

"No, it was her, I know it was her," she insisted, sure of what had occurred. "That dog has given me so many kisses over the years, it was exactly the same. I know it was her."

For several long moments, silence returned to the compartment of our vehicle. The only sound was the rhythmic reverberation of wipers working to clear raindrops from the windshield.

"Brandy wanted to let us know she's okay," my wife explained, breaking the silence. "That's why she licked me. To let us know that she's fine, that she's moved on, and waiting for us." The event comforted our mourning hearts and softened our sorrow.

The next morning we buried our precious pet as it lightly misted from the dreary, carbonized skies. We read liturgy from the Episcopal Prayer Book and offered prayers for her soul. We gave thanks for her thirteen years with us, each one good, happy, and healthy. Before closing the box for the final time, I placed a University of Tennessee Volunteers baseball cap on her furry head, one I often wore on cold mornings as we walked together in the woods. My wife also added several of the dog's favorite treats, and all of her play balls. There were many. Even during her last days, the dog played with those balls with the energy of a puppy.

The next evening our kindly church priest called to check in, having heard the news of our loss. We discussed animals and souls and heaven mostly. He assured us that the perfection of God's holy landscape was dotted with all kinds of creatures, especially pets. If God cared enough to make it, He would surely care enough to desire it in his heavenly kingdom. But this I already knew.

For on the rainy, dark night our dog left us, she also left a sign that she was still very much alive, a wet lick across my wife's neck, a canine kiss from a golden retriever we knew as Brandy.

David Michael Smith is a banker by day and a writer by night. He has been published multiple times and has written two novels. David enjoys sports, reading, and eating his wife's culinary creations.

An Angel Intervenes

by Andrew Hall

When I was a young man I fell in love with a girl named Teresa. She was going through a difficult divorce and had an infant to raise on her own. She was the first love of my life, and when things did not work out, I was devastated. It was a highly dysfunctional relationship, and we both behaved badly. But the ultimate fault was mine, and I am not proud of that.

After we broke up we continued to see each other from time to time. I had been living on my own in downtown Sacramento for about six months. Teresa would come and visit me now and again to see how I was doing. We'd make love, and talk about getting back together. I was trying to reform and she was trying to learn to trust me again.

At the time I was working two jobs to make ends meet. But with no car, it was not easy. I was riding my bicycle more than 100 miles a week to work and working more than 60 hours a week. With no overtime pay and all that exercise, food became more expensive than gas. I was struggling. I was getting even more depressed. I was feeling remorse for the things I did to Teresa and I was feeling worthless for the way I was living; barely making it.

One day I made some new friends. I like to play board games and the like with groups of people and these new friends were interested in learning to play so they invited me to their house. I came over, taking my bicycle. We played quite late at the house so they offered to let me stay the night on the couch; then I could head out in the morning fresh and in daylight. When I awoke, I found my bike was no longer locked to the stairs leading up to the apartment, where I had parked it the night before. That was my only way to get to work. That was a devastating blow.

Fortunately, the Salvation Army has bikes cheap; unfortunately, they have cheap bikes cheap. I bought the only bike I could afford there and it wasn't much. You can't imagine how much more difficult it is to ride a bike that isn't made for the distances I was riding and is in poor condition to boot. My trip times almost doubled. I was sleep deprived, irritable, and depressed. Even more demoralizing was the fact that I learned shortly afterwards that the friends who invited me over to teach them the game were the very people who stole my bicycle.

I lost faith in people, and well as in myself; feeling more and more alone, I slipped into the most terrible depression of my life. Suicide became a common thought. But I wasn't that far gone yet. One more event was to occur that would finally be that proverbial last straw that would forever change my life.

Teresa came to my apartment to visit me. She was very upset and began crying. I told her no matter what it was, she could tell me.

"This is the day that our child would have been born," Teresa said.

"What child?" I was in shock. I had no idea she had been pregnant.

As she explained it, she'd realized that she was pregnant while we were still living together, but never told me. After we broke up, she kept her pregnancy a secret from me, as there was so much bad blood between us at the time. Not long afterwards she'd had a miscarriage. The stress of our break-up and its aftermath had left her unable complete the pregnancy. At least that was what she'd said. Several times during our time together I'd warned her that if she got pregnant in order to trap me into marriage, I'd leave her. So part of me suspected that she'd had an abortion; that she didn't want to face me to tell me that she was pregnant after my telling her that I would leave her. I didn't know what to believe. But either way it was my fault.

A week later, on New Year's Day, I was on the phone with Teresa, trying desperately to make amends. She was still very ambivalent about me, and even though I was desperately crushed by her living away from me, and wanted us to live together again, there seemed to be no changing her mind. She was living with a man she told me was gay, but I had my suspicions. We argued about her moving back in with me, and the debate eventually came around to the topic of her roommate. When I asked her why her roommate exercised such influence on her decision making, she said, quite simply, "Because I love him."

"Oh." That's all I could think to say.

I had been so focused on making her happy so we could get back together that I had failed to see that all I had done these past few months was make her life more difficult. There was no point in my arguing with her as she was trying to move on from me and make a new life. I was still trying to hold on to something that no longer existed. I felt so horrible.

This, coupled with the realization that I had directly or indirectly cause the death of our child, finished me.

I had hurt the one woman who had truly loved me. She had no foul intentions towards me. Only wanted to help me, love me, nurture me, and care for me the way a loving woman might do. She was willing to share the raising of her daughter with me and trust me to raise her together. I had violated that trust. I had made parting ways so difficult that she was afraid to tell me that she was in a new relationship, for fear of retribution. I had destroyed her life, and caused the loss of another innocent life, and now my life was in the gutter. I had nothing left to live for.

It was time to end my life, I decided.

I took the last $100 from the last paycheck from a job I just lost due to my depression. I bought food for a last great feast, the likes of which I hadn't been able to afford for a long time. I bought two boxes of sleeping pills.

On Dec 31, 1996, I invited my friends over to play a game. We played games till eleven that night. It was a nice night. There was plenty of good food and we all had fun. After we were finished, I bid them all good night. I shook their hands and said goodbye. In my heart I would miss them. They left not knowing a thing. I sat down and with pencil and paper I wrote a note. I told whoever would read this that I was so sorry for what I'd done. The life I lead was not one I was proud of. I couldn't take back the things I did, so please God and people, forgive me. I then took both packs of sleeping pills and went to bed for the night, never planning to wake up again.

To say it went well, is to lie. I was terrified of what I had just done. I had a stuffed animal, a little bear, I held him tight and prayed. I prayed and I cried. I was so afraid. Strange things began to happen. Adrenalin, fear, the drugs I had consumed, I'm not sure, but I was not very aware of what was happening. Aside from all the strange things you may see after consuming so many pills, I saw one thing I will never forget. I closed my eyes and for a brief moment, I saw what I can only describe as large hands, a pair of them, opening before me. In these hands, a small child emerged.

My child.

Dazed, I went back to sleep for a very long time.

When I woke up, the phone was ringing. I was shocked to be alive. It was Wednesday. The sun was shining, it was noon. I had slept for 36 hours. Teresa called me. She wanted to know if everything was okay. She was worried about me and feared something happened to me. I told her what I had done.

I live right next door to my landlord. When I finally ventured outdoors, he spotted me and asked if I was okay. I said yes.

For the rest of my life, I will not know for sure what happened. All I know is that was the last time I ever hurt a living being with intention. Every once in a while I get the strangest feeling that I really did die and that this life is my punishment. Like climbing through the window to get out of the house instead of using the front door. Not a real difference on what you see, but rather on how you got there.

I have heard stories of people who hate their lives. Then one day something happens. A person changes overnight. Everyone they know sees this change; it's dramatic, but it's not conclusive. They say that sometimes a soul dies, but the body lives on. A body without a soul doesn't work, so it needs a new soul. I think my old soul left that day and a new one arrived to take over. Delivered by the hands of my own child, now an angel in heaven.

Thanks to that intervention, I'm changed forever and for the good.

Andrew Hall is a writer who works in the computer industry in San Jose, California. He's recently gone back to school to study anthropology.

Invisible Angels

by Patricia O'Donnell

*M*ommy," Lindsay said as she spooned her breakfast cereal, "there's an angel standing beside you." I looked up from the newspaper folded beside my plate.

"What are you talking about?"

My four-year-old daughter chomped her cereal. "Angel. There's an angel beside you." She finished her cereal and slid off the chair, only she forgot she was wearing roller skates, and her feet went in the air as she landed on her rear. I helped her up.

"Take your skates off now. It's time to go to daycare." In the car Lindsay leaned forward from the backseat, her face hanging above my shoulder.

"Lindsay, sit down and buckle your seat belt." She did. "Now tell me why you said you saw an angel this morning."

"Well!" She tried to lean forward again, but the belt held her back. "There was a light beside you, and angels are visible, so there could have been an angel there."

I remembered the sunlight striking the wall by my head, brighter now these early days of spring. "You mean invisible. Angels are invisible."

"Yes. Visible."

"Where did you learn about angels?" I asked.

"I forget."

I kissed Lindsay goodbye at the daycare, hoping that she would think no more about angels. I had never mentioned them to her—I was especially careful to avoid references to the supernatural of any kind. Children's natural trust is too often exploited, it seemed to me, causing grief and sorrow later on. I chose books for her that revealed the true wonders of the natural world rather than fairy tales, and I tried to avoid stories that had princesses being saved by the kiss or mighty sword of a prince. My daughter would grow up believing she could save herself, thank you. And there were certainly no angels apparent in my life, so why should I tell Lindsay there were?

At Rohner and Jacobson, Associates, where I was an architectural draftsperson (I clung to the title in spite of the difficulty Rohner had, continually referring to my colleague, Ed, and me as the "draftsmen"), the only angels that came into play were my own hard work and the monthly paycheck. I could refer to Ed as an angel, because he had taken me under his wing and generally done everything he could to help me become adjusted and successful at my job. I could call him an angel, but I wouldn't, because I knew that his kindness was that of a compassionate human.

When I arrived at the daycare after work, Lindsay was sitting in a corner by herself, looking through a book. Gloria, one of the teachers, motioned me into the other room.

"Something's wrong with that child today," she said. "She doesn't want to do anything. She just sat around, staring." Gloria always spoke with great emphasis.

"What do you think the problem is?"

Gloria shook her head and lowered her voice. "She wouldn't say, but I heard her talking about angels. Like she was talking to herself, you know?" Gloria looked at me over the top of her glasses. "Did you teach her about angels?" she asked sternly.

"No, I didn't. Do you talk about angels here?"

Gloria threw back her head and laughed. "No, no, we don't talk about any angels. The things these kids come up with!"

I approached Lindsay, holding her jacket. "Hi, honey. Time to go." I watched her slowly put on her jacket. When we were outside I asked, "How was your day?"

She walked carefully into a puddle of water and stood there, letting the ripples settle around the ankles of her rubber boots. "Okay."

"Just okay? What did you do?"

"Nothing."

"Lindsay, Gloria said you were quiet today and didn't want to do things. Is that right?"

"I don't know. I guess so."

"How come?"

She looked around in exasperation, then looked at me.

"Because of the angels," she said, raising her hands with fingers spread wide, as if she were explaining to a very small child. "I didn't want to make them mad." She stamped her foot in the water.

As I helped her into the car I asked, "Why would they get mad?"

"Because I'm not doing the right thing."

Enough was enough. "Lindsay," I said, "there are no angels, or fairies, or monsters. They are only pretend. Pretend. They never existed." I saw her face set as she looked ahead, kicking one boot out and back against the seat. "Is there anything else bothering you?" I asked, futilely imagining her answering in the same reasonable tone.

"We had broccoli for lunch today," she said angrily.

After supper I read while she played with dolls on the floor. I watched her as she bent down, a look of concentration on her chubby face. Her father used to get a similar expression on his face. He used to frighten me, at times, with his intensity. She took after him in ways not yet clear to me, and I hoped to direct her away from his passions and rages, to save her from disorder. Life need not be so difficult, I wanted to tell her.

I put down the book and stretched. Lindsay looked up suddenly from her play, her eyes unfocused. She was looking just beyond me, to the wall.

"Mommy . . ." she said.

"What?"

She looked at me then, and a guarded, secretive look came over her face.

"Nothing."

We read an alphabet book and Peter Rabbit (talking animals, I decided, were unavoidable in children's books). Lindsay was quiet, cuddling up with her blanket. I tucked her in and kissed her goodnight. After turning out the light I paused in the doorway, looking at her curled up in bed, thumb in mouth, and a blanket next to her ear.

Angels? What was next? Ghosts, witches, demons, and all intangible evils that cannot be fought, that cannot even be argued against because they are all invisible?

I tried to continue reading but felt restless, unable to concentrate. I poured a glass of wine from an open bottle in the refrigerator. With a second glass, I found myself digging through old journals and photograph albums. I found my pregnancy journal, with a description of the night I gave birth to Lindsay. She'd been early, and Lindsay's father—my ex-husband, Jack—was at a conference, unable to get home in time. Labor had been difficult, with no company except for nurses and the occasional visit from the doctor.

Sitting on the floor, the half-empty glass of wine beside me, I read the words I'd forgotten I wrote. Labor was getting intense and I was feeling really frightened, wishing Jack was there with me. The nurse was in and out. Suddenly, after a particularly rough contraction, I felt as if someone were near me. I was alone in the room, but it was as if someone else were there, someone strong and kind. I remembered then about breathing, and I knew that I would get through it. I didn't remember writing that, but I remembered labor, both the surprising pain and the joy on release. The strength I found somewhere.

I stretched, stiff from sitting on the floor for so long. It was late, and through half-opened curtains I saw a nearly full moon flickering through the trees.

When I finally fell asleep I dreamed of hiding in a dark house while unknown forces rattled doors and windows. In the dream I heard Lindsay crying somewhere. I found her upstairs, in a room bright with sunlight. Her face filled with joy, Lindsay pointed to a spot just beyond me, off to my left. I froze, terrified of what I would see if I turned, and woke with a start. The clock's face, glowing like a full moon in the dusky bedroom, let me know that it was nearly six. For some reason, the connection of the clock face with the moon lingered: face on the moon, the man in the moon, but the moon is a woman . . . the tides . . . I willed myself to be awake, to climb out of the clouds of unreason. I lay there a moment longer, but then I was drifting somewhere. I was floating with the waves, when I saw a face smiling up at me, round as a moon.

My alarm woke me. I got out of bed and splashed water on my face. I stared into the mirror, trying to see myself clearly, to see who I was. The face of a woman in her thirties met me, a startled-awake face, with faint shadows under wide-open eyes, and snarled hair. She looked real enough. If she's so grown-up, I asked myself, why do I feel like such a child sometimes? And if she's so real, why do I feel like a shadow, slipping in and out of who I'm supposed to be? My eyes shifted to the wall behind me, where the sun was lighting up the pale blue flowers of the wallpaper, touching them delicately.

Lindsay was awake in her bed, tousled brown hair falling over half-closed eyes and round cheeks.

"Good morning, pumpkin," I called in to her. In the kitchen I put on water for coffee, turned the radio to the classical music station, and pulled open the living room curtains. The morning light opened into the room just as a Bach sonata began, the complex interweaving violins filling the room. Perhaps it was the combination of sunlight and Bach, or the strangeness of my dreams and early morning thoughts, but at that moment I was overtaken by a sensation, a memory that had its roots somewhere in my body: the feeling of being in love—the way everything is changed, the way hope seems to permeate the air and the senses become charged, aware of color and beauty in ways previously forgotten.

I pushed the window up in its frame. I had to feel that cool morning air. It rushed in, touching my face and my bare arms against my nightgown. I could see the parking lot and house across the street, a few swaying trees tinged with green. The sky was in motion, grayish white clouds opening to let the sun through as if making a statement, then closing again to reconsider. The teenaged boy who lived across the street ran down the front steps, his jacket flapping. I felt the opening and closing of a door somewhere in the middle of my chest, the clean slap of wood on wood, a glimpse of darkened cool hallways.

There was the shuffle of slow footsteps, and Lindsay was by my side. She put one hand on my hip and stared out the window. A sudden shaft of sunlight seemed to penetrate her skin, illuminating it from the inside as if she were opaque. I touched her arm, her cheek. She looked at me curiously. I felt a lifting, a sudden shadow, and then the air was full of the sound of beating wings.

Patricia O'Donnell has had stories published in a number of publications, including The New Yorker. *She teaches fiction writing at the University of Maine at Farmington and lives in central Maine with her husband and daughter.*

Calling Out for Angels

by Davi Walders

*L*egend tells us that not all angels wanted humans created. Some felt that humans would be liars, while others thought that humans would be too quarrelsome. Legend also has it that God was not happy with the doubting angels and consumed them by the fire of His little finger. One angel named Labbiel, however, supported the creation of humans, and he was rewarded. His name was changed to Raphael, which means "God has healed," and he became head of the guardian angels and chief of the angelic order of virtues. His band of angels agreed to watch over humans and reveal their secrets to them. Raphael became the keeper of all medical remedies on earth.

We are sitting on Ann's balcony on a June evening, the one evening it hasn't stormed all spring, and we've reshuffled the small balcony to make room for her wheelchair so she can watch the sunset. With her sunglasses on, she holds her face up to the sun streaking the sky purple and orange over the cathedral. I move my chair to face her and I feel the warmth on my back.

"This feels good," she says, smiling and gazing from behind dark glasses out into the sky high above Washington DC. She sighs. "This balcony gives me so much pleasure."

Finally, she has allowed me to bring dinner and have a "girl's night out" on the balcony. She has been in a dark mood for weeks, considering another surgery for another part of her body gone wrong after a spinal stroke. She has decided against the surgery, even though she probably needs it. Perhaps the decision has called for a celebration of sorts, and this is why she has permitted me to join her. She sits with her Rob Roy, I with my glass of wine.

They say that Raphael sits behind those who are ill and in need. I keep hoping. Every day I pray for a change, a breakthrough. Still she sits in a wheelchair, this energetic friend whose high heels I can still hear clicking down the hallway in the school where we both taught. This intelligent woman, who left the teaching profession and entered the business world with remarkable entrepreneurial spirit, and had great success. Thank God she did. Who prepares for the financial drain of a spinal stroke in their fifties, let alone ever?

She is talking about old times, about the school where we met. About the "older" male teacher with the buzz cut who made us miserable until we filled his beakers with strange concoctions. The principal who wore white socks and was the terror of teenagers. We are laughing about it now as hard as we did thirty years ago. I am also keeping an eye out for Raphael, or at least an angel or two from his band of lesser angels who promised to watch over us.

I watch this brave friend, who has reworked her life with dignity each time parts of her body succumbed to different illnesses. I see how tired she is as she lifts herself with only the strength of her arms. "I have to stretch sometimes," she says. "Don't mind me." Hoisting herself up on the arms of the wheelchair, she locks her elbows.

"Can I help?" I ask. She shakes her head vehemently, dangles a moment, then lowers herself back into the wheelchair seat.

The conversation ebbs and flows. We talk about the investments we share with the same broker. I am cursing, she is laughing.

"Things have to get better," she says about the market. "It's all in the stars," she continues, admonishing me not to get so frustrated. I see my friend, this former science teacher turned astrologically minded businesswoman, chuckling in the sunset.

"It's chilly," I say. The sky is now only shades of blue and purple.

"Let's stay until the last bit of purple is gone," she says. "You know I love purple. I don't want to miss a moment of it."

"Your outfit matches the sky," I say, acknowledging her wardrobe that has been cleansed of everything but loose-fitting purple clothing—easy to get into and out of. We sit a moment longer. Finally she okays the move back inside, and we maneuver on the small balcony until she can push herself into the apartment.

I stand a moment longer, looking out over the cathedral into the dusky sky.

"What a heavenly night," she says, glancing back at the scattering of clouds still glistening above the cathedral. "What are you doing standing out there?" she asks. "You're the one who wanted to come inside."

"Raphael, where are the remedies?" I whisper out into the sky, my back turned, so my tough, tired friend can't hear.

"Come soon. If you're too busy, please send one of your lesser angels. Anything at all to help." I take one more look for signs in the sky. Knowing in my heart that angels have intervened for others, I follow the wheelchair into the apartment, awaiting our turn.

Davi Walders is a writer and educator whose poetry and prose have appeared in more than 150 publications. Her literary prizes include an Alden B. Dow Creativity Fellowship, a Maryland State Poetry Grant, and a Time-Out for Women Grant from the Association for Religion and Intellectual Life. She has been studying Jewish law and legends for many years.

Acknowledgments

The making of a book is a true collaboration in every sense of the word. Having written several books, and edited and designed more than we dare count, we can say without hesitation that there is an enormous amount of work going on behind the scenes—much more than the average reader is aware of.

There are many talented folks we'd like to thank for their time and effort in putting *Angel Over My Shoulder* together. For starters, we'd like to thank each of our wonderful contributors, a caring and unique group of individuals who had the foresight, hindsight, and gumption to tell their tales with candor and irrepressible charm and emotion. We know that for many of you, the excercise of putting your thoughts and scenarios to paper was a mentally and emotionally exhaustive effort. Both of us are extremely grateful—not to mention impressed—by your courage and professionalism in dealing with a challenge so personal in nature.

For the exceptional willingness you showed, and ultimately, the amazing stories you shared, we thank you from the bottom of our hearts. We sincerely hope the tribute and the catharsis your tales provide will help enlighten and encourage others to share their own experiences. May your angels keep you safe from harm and bring only the best to you and your families.

As we continually learn, angels come in many forms—in this case, publishing angels. We'd like to thank Fair Winds publisher Holly Schmidt for placing her faith in our angelic plan. Thanks, Holly! We look forward to working with you again very soon.

To our dear friend and Acquisitions Editor, Paula Munier (the consummate Blonde Bombshell), we offer a humble curtsy, unlimited cases of Kendall Jackson, and several additional decades of undying friendship and twisted humor. If angels do buzz the heavens, dear friend, you've got the luxury cadillac wings with all the extras! We couldn't have done it without you, on this celestial plane or any other. We love ya!

We'd also like to thank Managing Editor Brigid Carroll, whose wonderful wit and grace under pressure should never be underestimated. It's been a pleasure and privilege, my dear, and rest assured, there will always be a margarita (or twenty) with your name on it at the Karg/Sutherland abode.

Also part of the Fair Winds family is Art Director Claire MacMaster, who we'd like to thank for her diligence and dedication during the production process. We'd also like to thank Editorial Assistant Rhiannon Soucy, who spent many hours perusing our angelic prose and offering sound advice and editing, and copy editor Karen Levy who did a fabulous job pulling things together. Many thanks to you both!

Back home in Oregon, we have the honor of working with Ellen Weider, a brilliant editor, proofer, and researcher who also took a turn with the our angel endeavor. What can we say? In a town where the most exciting occurrence is a new burrito in the Texaco deli, you help remind us on a daily basis that there *is* intelligent life on the planet. You do it so well in fact, that we'd put major bucks on you in a professional Scrabble tournament. You're the bomb baby!

As always, we'd like to acknowledge Natasha and the rest of the fine folks who comprise the Arttoday.com family. The service you provide us graphic designers is simply the best.

Lastly, we'd like to thank our respective families who never cease to amaze us with their love and support, no matter how nutty our undertakings, how twisted our collective wits, or how eccentric our lifestyle. We got lucky in this lifetime, because we couldn't ask for a better bunch. Our love always, to each one of you.

In closing, we wanted to share one final thought that is never far from either of us. In a world that is often saturated by chaos and dysfunction, it's a comfort to know that light, honor, intelligence, and humor can ultimately prevail. Revealing unusual encounters isn't always the easiest of tasks, even amid a gaggle of "open minded" individuals. But true courage comes from within. From speaking one's mind and telling a story with grace and aplomb—simply by accepting the notion that anything is possible.

It happens to us on a daily basis, and we wish you all the best on your own journeys . . . wherever they may lead.

On the following page is a drawing by Amber Handy, the talented young daughter of contributor Jerri Handy. She draws angels, and as you can see, everything is possible.

A heartfelt thanks and best wishes to you all.

—*Barb Karg and Rick Sutherland*

by Amber Handy

Also from Fair Winds Press

YOUR GUARDIAN ANGEL IN A BOX
by Reverend Kimberly Marooney
ISBN: 1-931412-39-1
$26.95 (£16.99)
Kit; 256 pages
Available wherever books are sold

You are never alone.

Your guardian angel is always beside you—all day, every day, for all the days of your life.

With this benevolent and loving spirit to guide and protect you on your spiritual journey, you'll navigate life's twists and turns with faith and hope. Inspired and motivated by your guardian angel, you'll find you can live life more fully—and more meaningfully.Invoke your guardian angel—and you'll develop a relationship with the heavenly messenger who's always been there for you—and always will be.

With this lovely kit, you can develop a closer relationship with your guardian angel. Reverend Kimberly Marooney, the best-selling author of *Angel Blessings*, shows you how to commune with the angelic spirit sent to protect you and guide you through all your days on Earth. Through sacred counsel with your personal messenger from God, you will lead a more spiritually fulfilling and meaningful life.

Inside:
• Beautiful angel statue
• Elegant angel pin
• *The Seven Gifts of Your Guardian Angel*, a 256-page book about connecting with your guardian angel
• Keepsake box that can be used as an altar

ANGEL BLESSINGS
By Kimberly Marooney
ISBN: 1-931412-55-3
$35.00 (£19.99)
Kit; 160 pages
44 full-color cards
Available wherever books are sold

Angel Blessings was created as a powerful oracle for the Journey of the Heart and as a pathway to our spiritual Home. This deluxe book and card gift set enables you to have a more flowing, healing, and loving connection with the Angelic Kingdom.

There are 44 Angel Blessing cards, each one a beautiful reproduction of a fine art masterpiece inscribed with the name of the Angel and the Angel's mission. The artwork has been carefully selected to convey the feeling and essence of each Angel, drawing from the work of such masters as Rembrandt, van Gogh, Lippi, Raphael, Frangelico, and Blake.

The 160-page guidebook offers an in-depth description of all the Angels showing you how to manifest each one's essence in your life. There are nine different ways to work and play with the cards ranging from single card drawings to more involved processes. All of the sacraments and spreads are designed to connect us with the sacredness of our spiritual communications, feelings, and visions.

The Angels are messengers of Healing, Peace, Forgiveness, Love, Courage, and Prosperity.

Reverend Kimberly Marooney is an angel expert and the author of *Your Guardian Angel in a Box*. A fourth-generation minister, Kimberly devotes her life to helping others experience the personal presence of angels in their lives. She lives in Southern California.